To the
D1645015
AUSTRIA
ITALY
Lienz
Brunico
Val Pusteria
Dobbiaco
Sillian
Drava Valley
2750
LIENZ DOLOMITES
Lago di Braies
V. d. Landro
F. Rienza
CRODA DI BECCO 2890
3139 CRODA ROSSA
2998 CIME DI LAVAREDO
3092 C. UNDICI
C. DODICI 3094
MONTE CROCE PASS
SASS RIGAIS 3025
Val Badia
CRISTALLO 3216
Misurina
Auronzo
San Stefano di Cadore
LE TOFANE 3243
Corvara In Badia
Cortina
3151
NUVOLAU 2648
3205 SORAPIS
MARMAROLE 2932
2709 CRODA DA LAGO
M. ANTELEO 3263
Pieve di Cadore
Ampezzo
MARMOLADA 3342
3168 PELMO
Álleghe
3228 CIVETTA
Val di Zoldo
Cencenighe
Ospitale
N
COLLE PASS
C. D. VEZZANA 3191
Ágordo
Longarone
PALA DI SAN MARTINO 2996
Fiera di Primiero
Ponte nelle Alpi
Belluno
Road
Railway
Peak with height in metres 2701
Main junctions
Small places
Scale 0 5 10 15 20 KMS.
0 5 10 MILES
Feltre
Vittorio Veneto
To Treviso and Venice
To Treviso and Venice
L.R.

THE DOLOMITES

By the same Author:

Rock for Climbing
Mountain Photography
Making Lantern Slides and Film Strips

The Sella Inn—Gröden Dolomites

THE DOLOMITES

by

C. Douglas Milner

Member of the Alpine Club, etc.
Fellow of the Royal Photographic Society

With 150 illustrations
by the author and
7 map-diagrams

London

Robert Hale Limited

18 Bedford Square W.C.1

First published 1951

PRINTED AND BOUND IN GREAT BRITAIN BY
WILLIAM CLOWES AND SONS, LIMITED, LONDON AND BECCLES

Contents

Illustrations

GROUP I—*continued*

GROUP II

GROUP II—*continued*

GROUP III

GROUP III—*continued*

GROUP IV

GROUP IV—*continued*

GROUP V

GROUP VI

Introduction

THIS book is a general introduction to this superb district of the Eastern Alps. It is essentially a book for the fireside rather than the rucksack, and does not seek to replace the excellent modern guidebooks mentioned in the Bibliography, written in either German or Italian. Still less does it compete with that much abused, but indispensable, pocket guide in English, Baedeker's *Tyrol and the Dolomites.*

It is hoped that the photographs will give pleasure to readers who already know the district, and encouragement to those who are disposed to pay it a visit. Photographers will be interested to learn that all have been taken with miniature cameras, about half of them on 35-mm. size.

The simplified map-diagrams are intended to give a general picture of each group, and the detailed maps mentioned in the Bibliography are advised for closer study.

My source books, particularly for the history of mountaineering, are quoted on page 97, and I am especially glad to acknowledge a great debt to the *Alpine Journal.*

As the reader may deduce from certain of the illustrations, my evaluations of dolomite climbing, up to and including Grade V, are not entirely based on theory.

The *sesto grado* is another matter. I do not trouble it, and it does not trouble me. It would be orthodox for an English climber to declaim against "steeple-jack" methods, but the new style is much less obtrusive than the publicity given to it suggests. In any case, it is a pursuit for the local expert rather than the foreign visitor. Let the boys have their fun. Climbers who are interested in the *sesto grado* will find an excellent summary of its manifestations in the Dolomites in the 1950 edition of Berti's *Dolomiti Orientali*, whilst the great Comici has told of his own adventures and attitude to mountains in *Alpinismo Eroico*. There are numerous other volumes available in German and Italian, as well as notices of new climbs in *Der Bergsteiger* and the *Rivista Mensile* of the Italian Alpine Club.

* * * *

As always, my wife has given me invaluable help at every stage of the book.

C. DOUGLAS MILNER.

November 1950.

The Spinney,
Upton, Wirral.

The Dolomite Mountains

THE Dolomites are among the strangest and most beautiful rock peaks in the world. They are neither vast and high like the rock peaks among the Himalaya, the American Rockies, or even the Swiss Alps, nor are they so minute by world standards as the crags of the British hills. Few summits are more than ten thousand feet above sea-level, yet often between a third and a half of that height is occupied by massive rock walls and towers with large areas of continuously vertical cliff. Their strangeness lies not only in their steepness or the many fantastic pinnacles among them, but also in their colouring of golden yellow and grey, streaked and flecked at times with black and purple and red, with dazzling white scree slopes at their foot.

In parts they seem bare and desolate by comparison with the mossy and richly tinted crags of Britain; and their effect of ruined masonry, of having been thrown up almost crudely is, in its detail, less attractive than the sweeping sculptured lines of the granite peaks such as the Aiguilles of Chamonix.

Sometimes, in the glare of noonday, such eccentric creations can look less like mountains than the residual bleached skeletons of mountains that long ago have died, ghostly and terrible in their arid silence. No streams run through the upper glens; there is no grass or tree growth; no sound is to be heard; and only the climber who loves both solitude and bare rock can be fully at ease among them.

But the dramatic lines of the outer bastions of a Dolomite fortress exist for all to enjoy, as they rise swiftly from the hillslopes above the green forests and the flowery Alpine meadows at their feet, to sparkle against the deep blue Italian skies. Above all they react to fine conditions of atmosphere and weather. They are a superb stage setting for the beauty that can be created by the light of dawn and sunset, by the march of a storm, by the wind-blown mists, and by the round of the seasons. A red sunrise can be as exquisite among these crags as upon any great ice peak. Then the roses bloom upon all of them and not merely, as the legend has it, on the Rosengarten, the rose garden of Laurin the Goblin King. As the storm-wrack shreds out among the pinnacles, some of the mountain landscapes revealed are incomparable in splendour.

The Dolomites are a very small part indeed of the eastern limestone Alps, which in all are spread over an area as large as Switzerland, stretching from the shores of Lake Constance to the Raxalpe near Vienna in the east, from Bavaria in the north to the Julian Alps of Yugoslavia. All limestone is distinguished by its boldness of form. That can be seen even in Britain: at the Cheddar Gorge, the Winnats Pass, and the Derbyshire Dales. It can be seen abroad in the high face of the Watzmann in Bavaria and in the ridges of the Jura. But dolomite is a special kind of limestone, containing magnesium as well as calcium, and is much harder and also more colourful than "mountain" or carboniferous limestones. As a layman and not a geologist, I would say that it stands midway between limestone and marble, in its incipient translucence and the polish it can acquire. It is rarely seen in mountain crests and is more common as a quarry stone. Much of the beauty of Venice lies in the use of this magnesian limestone, whilst the one true, if unrecognised, dolomite campanile in England is the tower of Big Ben, whose stone came from the Bolsover quarries in Derbyshire. In that county, at least, there is one tiny exposed rock face of dolomite. At Brassington Rocks, those who have fallen under the spell of the Dolomites of the South Tyrol can lay their hands once again upon the rough rock, feel the grip of rubbers or *kletterschuhe*, and for a little time recapture the thrills of those airy walls that soar into the sky.

* * * *

The majority of the Dolomite Mountains are concentrated into a rectangle of north-east Italy between the valleys of the Adige in the west and the Piave in the east, bounded on the south by the Val Sugana and on the north by the Val Pusteria (Pusterthal). It would be unjustifiable to exclude from this book one other compact group just outside this rectangle, the Brenta, west of the Adige, which some climbers regard as perhaps the finest of all.

A few Dolomites are found elsewhere, but are not included in this book. North-east of the Val Pusteria, just across the Austrian border, are the smaller

. The Trentino Hills from Lombardy
:. Limestone Walls of the Adige Valley

3. Torre Civica, Trento

4. Piazza Cesare Battisti, Trento
5. San Lorenzo, and the Monument to Cesare Battisti

6. Under the Duomo, Trento
7. Near the Duomo, Trento

3. Frescoed Walls, Trento

9. The Piazza, Bolzano (Bozen)
10. Morning in Bolzano

. Old Bolzano, with the Gothic Spire
. War Damage in Bolzano (1946)

13. The Fruit Market, Bolzano
14. The Brenner Road, North of Bolzano

15. The Benedictine Cloister of Saben
16. The Village below it: Chiusa (Klausen)

17. The First Dolomites: Latemar Group from Caressa al Lago (Karersee)
18. The Catinaccio (Rosengarten) from Caressa al Lago

. Rizzi's Inn at Vigo di Fassa
. In the Val di Fassa

21. Fontanazzo with its Campanile
22. The Val di Fassa, with the Pordoi Pass

Canazei, the Last Village in the Val di Fassa
24. The Sasso Pordoi from the Pass

25. Punta Grohmann and Cinque Dita (Grohmannspitze and Fünffingerspitze) from the Pordoi Pass

6. The Civetta and the Cordevole Valley from Arabba
7. Below the Dolomite Road at Livinallongo

28. Cortina d'Ampezzo—the End of the Road
29. A Branch Road—the Sella-Canazei

peaks of Lienz; in Switzerland there is the group near the Splügen—the Piz d'Aela, Tinzenhorn, and Piz Michel; in the Dauphiné are the dolomitic peaks of the Royannais, Vercors, and Devoluy districts, oddly enough very near to the home of Déodat de Gratet, Marquis de Dolomieu, whose researches in the real Dolomites led to his discovery of the distinctive character of the limestone rock, for which de Saussure suggested the name of *dolomie* in his honour. Yet the Marquis, his eyes fixed on a more distant prospect, entirely missed his home Dolomites. In a similar way Sir Humphry Davy, preoccupied with the prospect of good fishing in Carinthia, passed by the Dolomites and assumed them to be granite.

Holidays in the Dolomites

THE palmy days of the Dolomites for travellers were probably at the turn of the century, and in the years before the Great War. Germany and Austria were as prosperous as Britain and America, and between the four of them this great holiday ground was well used, especially in the Cortina district. Discriminating people, such as the late W. A. Baillie-Grohmann, deplored the spoliation of many of the more accessible parts by the excessive zeal of the *Deutscher und Oesterreichischer Alpenverein* and similar large-scale organisations in making club paths. In the south much was lost of remoteness by the construction of military roads as part of the Austrian defensive outworks, culminating in the Dolomitenstrasse (1907). But it was left to the Italians after the war to continue the process of road-making begun by the Austrians, also partly as military counter-defences, but with the added desire to promote *il turismo* in a motoring age.

For my own part, I do not think these roads are so great a misfortune as is sometimes assumed, certainly much less than one or two road projects in the Lake District would be, where the region is so much smaller. But if the Italians, in their preference for the ease and safety of road touring, have developed these highways, they have allowed (by casualness perhaps rather than by design) many of the more objectionable improvements in the mountain paths to fall into a decent decay, so that at the present time there is probably less to complain of than there was forty years ago. Here and there is still a discordant feature—for instance, the signpost on the Bocca di Brenta is one of the things that the C.A.I. should remove. But in general the traveller is left to enjoy a land of beauty, if he chooses to be so left, rather than directed to a series of beauty spots. With the exception of the few obvious tourist centres, which include San Martino, Madonna di Campiglio, and Cortina, the majority of villages and towns seem to have a little tourist industry superimposed upon a fundamentally more significant range of normal agricultural activities, fruit growing, viniculture, dairying, lumbering. There is here in the Dolomites much less of the "magnificently bogus", of carefully restored ancient monuments, and of the over-commercialised type of catering for tourists that in so many parts of Switzerland is carried through with the unrelenting thoroughness, if not entirely with the arrogance, of the Teuton. Today, in the year 1950, it is still possible to find quiet valleys which recall what Amelia Edwards said in 1873:

> "It is difficult to speak of the people, the climate, of the scenery, without risk of being thought too partial or too enthusiastic . . . it is as natural to the natives of these hills and valleys to be kind and helpful and disinterested, as it is to the Swiss to be rapacious—to say that here one escapes from hackneyed sights; from over-crowded hotels; from the dreary routine of tables d'hôte; from the flood of Cook's tourists—is, after all, but to say that life in the South-Eastern Tyrol is yet [more or less] free from all the discomforts that have of late years made Switzerland unendurable, and that for those who love sketching and botany, mountain-climbing and mountain air, and who desire when they travel to leave London and Paris behind them, the Dolomites offer a playground far more attractive than the Alps."

The district is compact, and perfectly adapted for general travel either by road or on foot. Yet there is much to be said for staying in one region and enjoying a blend of the three different types of personal exploration available. First, the things that lie close at hand; the villages and their peoples, the country scenes, the ancient churches and castles. Second, the upland walking over the alps, through the forests, and among the mountains. Third, and most remarkable of all, the climbing of the peaks, and the enjoyment of the sport of rock-climbing in all its wide range of difficulty on the steepest and most thrilling faces of rock that are to be found in the world.

Road Travel

It is a serious business to take a car from England halfway across Europe to tour the district, but if it is done the best approach is through Switzerland via the Engadine, by the Ofen and Stelvio passes, down the Val Venosta to Merano and Bolzano. In this way the fine peaks of the Ortler are well seen, whilst such survivals as old Schloss Tirol at Merano can be visited. It is one of the most fascinating of the hundreds of Tyrolese strongholds of the Middle Ages. From Bolzano, a fine centre for the western hills, many roads are open. Over the pass to La Mendola, with its distant prospects of the Brenta, only two hours' driving away; up the valley to Chiusa and Bressanone and Fortezza with their castles and palaces; down the valley to Trento. Or if a quiet countryside is sought, it can be found in the Val Gardena, the Val di Non, or the Val di Fassa.

In the east Cortina is the obvious choice as a centre. From here the few but excellent lakes of the Dolomites can be visited. The Lago di Landro, the Lago d'Alleghe, Misurina, or even the remoter Lago di Braies (Pragser Wildsee) by the Val Pusteria (Pusterthal).

A longer tour from Cortina by the southern rim of the mountains brings in Pieve di Cadore, birthplace of Titian; historic Belluno; the gorges of the Val Sugana; and from there the ideal approach to remote Primiero.

But the man who is not so fortunate as to be able to travel by private car in this attractive way still has very many of these towns within his reach. The choice of a few centres, with very little walking from each, will still bring to him much of the best the Dolomites have to show.

Railroad transport in the region is limited in its range. The Brenner line is valuable, with its branches to Merano, the Val di Fiemme, and the Val Pusteria. The Val Sugana line from Trento links up in the south-east with the Venice–Cortina railroad. The electric line from there to the Val Pusteria is also worth using: it passes along the Lago di Landro and up to Dobbiaco.

But the popular and comfortable way to travel around and within the Dolomites is by bus.

Modern motor travel in the Dolomites is excellently organised, mainly by the S.A.D. (Societa Automobilistica Dolomiti), whose big coaches with their trumpet horns are seen and heard on every road of importance.

Not only is it convenient to travel in this way from such distant places as Milan, Venice, St Moritz, or Innsbruck to Bolzano or Cortina, but the local services are also excellent. It is possible to encircle the whole region from Trento, up the Brenner, along the Val Pusteria, down to Cortina, Belluno, and the Val Sugana.

The three main roads into the Dolomite region from this circle are: the great Dolomite Road from Bolzano to Cortina; the branch road through the Val Gardena, over the Sella Pass and down to Canazei; the branch road leaving the Val Sugana at Primolano to Primiero and San Martino then passing over the Rolle Pass to the Val di Fassa at Predazzo.

By these main arteries any centre can easily be reached, whilst large mountain masses lie between the road systems. It would be orthodox to mourn the disappearance of the mules the early travellers rode across the passes; the old, slow *stellwagen* of the north; or the more elegant *einspanner* of the 'nineties. But there are compensations. The visitor from England, with only two or three weeks to spare, finds it pleasant, and perhaps not unromantic, to climb a peak at Cortina in the morning, catch the afternoon coach, and dine in Bolzano. Or on a rest day at San Martino, to go down to Venice by the early coach, spend a day among the glories of its architecture, and yet be back in the cool mountain air before bedtime.

Quite apart from the advantage of getting somewhere in particular, the journeys themselves are often magnificent. Admittedly, in the best valleys, it is necessary for the sunshine roof of the coach to be open if the mountain tops are to be seen, but when the view palls—if it ever does—the remarkable *verve* of the drivers in taking corners at speed on roads clinging to crags above deep gorges ensures that imaginative passengers do not succumb to boredom.

Most of the longer routes are only in service from July to September, but all the villages are served somehow, by *autocorriere*, at other times, and the out-of-season visitor is thus not impeded, though travel needs more careful planning. These postal buses remind one strongly of the Scottish motor services beyond the Glen, with their mixed loads of passengers and luggage.

History along the Roads

THE Dolomite region is steeped in historical associations, of which abundant traces remain. If you look out from the balcony at the top of the Campanile di San Marco in Venice on a clear day, over the towers and red-tiled roofs of that beautiful city, across the plain of Venezia, you can sometimes see on the horizon other campaniles and towers that are the mountains. They mark the outer limits of the land possessions of the great mediæval republic, for Primiero, Belluno, Caprile, and Cortina were once Venetian.

On the other side of the mountains the western approach to the Dolomites can be made by the most historic highway in Europe—the Brenner road from Verona, at the gate of Lombardy, running north over the pass to Innsbruck, a centre of all that is finest in Germanic civilisation. This road along the broad valley of the Adige has been the link between the Latin and German peoples since the days of Rome.

Its earliest recorded history begins with the campaigns of Drusus against such Alpine tribes as the Brixentes and Rhætii, and Pons Drusi is the ancient name of Bolzano. In later years the whole valley, as well as its lateral branches, was colonised and Trento (Tridentum) was a flourishing town.

Down the same road came the conquering Visigoths and Vandals, Ostrogoths and Alemani. After the decline of the Lombard kingdoms, curious enclaves remained. On the one hand, in the obscure lateral valleys such as the Gardena and Ladinia (Gröden and Gaderthal) remnants of the early Roman settlers remained. Later ebbs and flows of conquest and colonisation left the Germanic villages of the Val di Non, or of the Setti Communi east of Trento, where a German patois has died out only in the last fifty years.

In the Dark Ages, between 800 and 1400, more than sixty journeys were made along this road by Holy Roman Emperors from the northland. The city of Trento, important in Roman times, grew even greater as capital of the province, the seat of a Prince Bishop. The immediate surroundings of Bolzano, the next strategic point at the junction of the Etsch (Adige), the Eisack (Isarco), and the Talfer (Talvera) became the site of numerous baronial strongholds, as indeed did the whole valley. Beyond the Isarco gorge above Bolzano grew Bressanone (Brixen), another capital of a Prince Bishop.

The Isarco gorge itself in the early centuries carried little more than a narrow track alongside the river, and the Roman carriage-road was built high on the hillsides to avoid it. But in 1314 one Kunter, an enterprising citizen of Bolzano, made the track which bears his name; and a century and a half later the Count of Tyrol, in whose lands it lay, used gunpowder to blast away crags and so make possible a better cart-road. But not until 1772 was a modern carriage-road made, and the gorge must have been a serious obstacle to the long trains of baggage wagons that followed the travelling companies of soldiers and notables who used the road.

The Brenner railway, built in 1864–7, was the first to cross the Alpine chain, and does so, of course, without a tunnel. Had it been completed before the Austro-Italian War of 1866, when the Venetian province was lost to Austria, the fighting might have been more severe, for it would have enabled the Austrians to bring large armies direct to Trento and the Val Sugana.

Today a journey from Verona to Bolzano and the Brenner is enriched by some such recollections of its colourful history. Moreover, this approach is a very convenient one to travellers who are intending to visit the Western Dolomites by rail from Switzerland. There is little to choose in time between the Simplon–Orient Express line from Calais to Verona and the northern approach through Germany and Austria via Innsbruck to Bolzano.

The northern part of the Lombardy Plain, with its endless leagues of maize and corn, vineyards and mulberry fields, gives no hint of the great limestone peaks hidden away to the north beyond the faint line of foothills that stand behind the incredibly blue Lake of Garda, or beyond the towers of Verona or Vicenza. But once the international railway is left at Verona, the vineyards and orchards begin to rise in terraced hillsides, and the first limestone cliffs are seen flanking the narrow Chiusa di Verona, guarded by a steep rock on which stands the famous Castle of Rivoli. Hereabouts was fought one of the more important battles of Napoleon's Italian campaigns, and it was from this castle that Masséna, a Marshal of the Empire, took his title.

The valley opens out more before Trento is reached, when once again the limestone cliffs arise as a foretaste of the Dolomites proper. These cliffs are similar in colour and vigour of form, but are only partly made of the true dolomite. They make an imposing background to the towers and castles of this beautiful city. It has clearly been Italian in character for many centuries, and although from 1814 to 1919 it was in Austrian territory, there is little evidence of this long occupation. It is graced by an ancient cathedral and many other fine churches, among which is Santa Maria Maggiore, famous as the meeting-place of the eighteen-year Council of Trent, where the principles of the Counter-Reformation were evolved and the final breach between Protestants and Catholics was created in the curse upon all heretics pronounced by the presiding Cardinal.

In its spacious piazzas, tall shuttered buildings, shadowed arcades, as well as in its great churches, Trento has all the mellowness of a city that has survived many wars and known many different rulers. The great rock above the city, Doss Trento, was a fort under the Romans, and the city was later occupied and developed by the Ostrogoths under Theodoric, taken by the Lombards, again by the Franks, attacked by the Venetians, and involved in Napoleon's campaigns. It was fortunate to miss the destruction that might have come its way, even in the war of '66, but the armistice prevented the Italians advancing up the Val Sugana from reaching it. Again it escaped the fate of French or Flemish cities in the Great War, for the Austrian line was held some miles below the city, and the Italians never succeeded in advancing.

In the recent war too it escaped the destruction from the air that overcame so much of the ancient southern parts of Italy. It was certainly bombed, as was almost every other point of importance up the whole Brenner line. But it was impossible to pass through all these places in 1946 or 1947 without admiring the great accuracy of the air attack that had to be made. Whilst every bridge, every railway station was demolished, damage was very concentrated. In Trento the railway station was destroyed (it has been handsomely rebuilt in the last two years), but "near misses" of this objective have luckily fallen so as to avoid the great cathedral and other fine buildings. One hit near the station at least opened up the view on Plate 5, and the memorial to Cesare Battisti can be seen in the background, on Doss Trento, whilst the romanesque church of San Lorenzo stands unharmed.

Cesare Battisti was a hero of *Italia Irredenta.* A deputy in the Imperial Diet of the old Austro-Hungarian Empire, and a native of Rovereto near Trento, he left Austria before she entered the Great War, to take a commission in the Italian Army. He was captured by the Austrians, who promptly (and properly) shot him as a traitor. To the Italians he is equally properly a hero, and his memory is kept fresh not only by this magnificent tomb but by the present name of the main square, formerly the Piazza del Duomo, later the Piazza Vittore Emmanuele III, and now the Piazza Cesare Battisti. Despite the Austrian-Nazi occupation of the Adige, it is interesting that they left his monument untouched, even in the retreat.

This wide square, flanked by the Duomo on one side, by the Pretorio on another, and with tall houses elsewhere, is a feature and focus of the city. Above the houses rises the tower of Santa Maria Maggiore (Plate 4), and the flamboyant frescoes of one old façade, near the Neptune Fountain, are reproduced on Plate 8. The cobbled road here, which has felt the tread of marching armies, of the horses and carriages of many centuries, and of the advancing jeeps of the Allied Forces, is again left to the cyclists of modern Italy and to the big Lancia coaches of the S.A.D., who maintain the postal services to the neighbouring valleys, as well as carrying travellers to all parts of the Trentino.

* * * *

But whatever destination in the mountains we may be seeking, Trento is an excellent halting place on the long, hot journey from England.

With the setting of the sun, the blanket of heat is lifted, the high crags of Monte Bondone fade into the sky, and in the cool comfort of an Italian summer's evening we can here sit at coffee under the oleanders of the pleasant squares, or under the dropping branches of the trees in the boulevards, and watch the lights of the Innsbruck express as it passes along the valley towards San Michele and Bolzano.

Trento has long connections with the exploration of the Dolomites (see page 68), for here and at Rovereto were many members of the *Vecchia e gloriosa,* Societa degli Alpinisti Tridentini, the Italian club established in Austrian territory so long ago as 1873, and responsible for much pioneering work in the Brenta and to a less extent in other areas.

* * * *

When the northward journey is resumed after a rest in Trento, the fascination of the valley scenery again makes the route a pleasant one. Incidentally, much more can be seen from a comfortable slow train to Bolzano than from either the electric expresses or the motor coaches. The steep hills still rise across the valley, slopes of arid scrub vegetation alternating with vertical cliffs, of the type that inspired Dante with his visions of the Inferno, for it was in this valley that he lived for some years. Villages of close-set houses, with low pantiled roofs, stucco walls, and the inevitable tall campanili of their churches, are set among the rich fields at either side of the river; here and there a small castle gleams on its crag as a memory of the once powerful barony of the Etschthal, as it was called, before it became the Adige. The river itself is controlled or diverted both for irrigation and for the powerful hydro-electric installations that the Italians have brought into being since they acquired the country.

Between Trento and Bolzano are the villages of Welsch Metz and Deutsch Metz, names dating from the time of the Lombard kings, but now rechristened Mezzo Corona and Mezzo Lombardo. The old names, where *Welsch* is a Germanic word for "foreign", and especially for "Italian", show that here was a line of demarcation between Italian and Germanic peoples. (Similarly there were Welschnofen and Deutschnofen above Bolzano, the former on the Dolomite Road being known today as Nova Levante.)

The tall limestone crags again fade out of the landscape near Bolzano; the valley becomes much wider and more open, bounded by red porphyry cliffs with pine forests rising to them on the northern and eastern slopes. The vineyards are still seen, but they are increasingly replaced by vast orchards, for here around Bolzano are the best fruit lands of Europe. The apple, peach, plum, nectarine, greengage, and cherry and many other fruits grow to perfection, and the fruit market of the town of Bolzano is famous, whilst the big growers or the co-operative syndicates have an important export trade from this region.

Bolzano is as fundamentally, even aggressively, Austro-Tyrolese as Trento is Italianate. The Gothic churches look over old narrow streets where Austrian names and black-letter signboards are the rule. The steeper roofs speak rather of the snowy northland and Alpine climate of Austria than of the Mediterranean heat and mild winter of Lombardy. The police and officials may be Italian, but they move among inhabitants whose appearance is often identical with that of the blond Austrian or the stocky, black-haired Alpine peoples of Tyrol. The white stocking, symbol of German culture (in a good sense), the leather shorts, are seen here at times, yet in Trento not at all. Comparison of Plate 9, the Platz of Bozen, with Plate 4, the Piazza of Trento, will illustrate the difference in appearance between the two cities, and the old red granite church with its openwork spire crowns the Gothic aspect of the city (Plate 11).

Once again, how accurate the bombing was, and how carefully limited to what was the minimum necessary to keep the road and railway impassable. The church has survived, though one other is destroyed, and Plate 12 shows one block of buildings on the main road, possibly of the Mussolini-renaissance style, that has been hit.

From the upper windows of Bolzano I first saw the Dolomites in the glitter of morning light. I had travelled straight out from England just after the recent war, in one exhausting journey of forty continuous hours by train, and stayed at the Victoria near the station. Next morning, quite unexpectedly, beyond the roofs of the city in a bright morning sky was a distant saw-toothed ridge and at one point, unmistakable in blue silhouette, were the Vajolet Towers. These famous pinnacles, so small and remote, were at that moment even more thrilling to my mind than had been the faint white dome of Mont Blanc seen from the heights of the Jura over the morning mists after a separation of nine years from the Alps.

The ideal time of day to see this long ridge of the Rosengarten (I shall never become reconciled to Catinaccio, the cacophonous Italian name for the mountain) is in the evening when the rocks glow with the light of the dying sun. Even better than an upper room in Bolzano is the pleasant upland of the Renon (Ritten), and from its pine groves or over its meadows the view eastwards is of a long line of the Dolomite crags above the porphyry hills. It is easy to see how this marvellous colouring of sunset created among the Tyrolese peasants of long ago the Legend of the Rose Garden. The Legend exists in various forms, and as I do not think any book on the Dolomites (with the exception of climbers' guides, where reliance on legend is unwise) has ever omitted some account of the curious goings-on which are supposed to have occurred, I feel compelled to repeat the main details. The account is as brief as I can make it, strictly derivative, and offered without responsibility on my part or on the part of my publishers.

The Garden of Roses was the sole possession above ground of Laurin, King of the Dwarfs. He was, in general, not well disposed to humans, but desiring a human wife he carried off Simild of Styria, and was promptly attacked by her brother Dietlieb, with his friends Dietrich of Bern (he of the *Nibelungenlied*) and Hildebrand. The dwarf counter-attacked with magic, drugging the heroes, who were rescued by Simild. They then slaughtered Laurin and his dwarfs, laid waste to the garden, and the skeleton peaks of the Rosengarten range are all that remain.

Should the serious reader feel, as well he may, that the horns of Elfland are blowing a little too faintly from this bald abstract, I advise him to stay, when in Bolzano, at the Albergo del Rey Laurino. This hotel is in many ways no better than the many other excellent hotels in Bolzano, indeed throughout the Dolomites, but it has a unique series of grotesque murals of the Legend by a modern Munich artist. With a little leisure, a bottle of Chianti, and these pictures, the stirring period of the *Nibelungenlied* and the *Heldenbuch* can perhaps be captured more easily. (The local brandy, *Grappa*, will produce not only pink roses but also pink dwarfs.)

Bolzano has more to offer than fruit, wine, and the Legend. It has its arcades of good shops, and many stores can be laid in here before starting for the Dolomite interior. Deficiencies of climbing or walking kit, such as boots and *kletterschuhe*, or spare soles of the special felt, are best bought here rather than at Cortina or the small villages among the mountains. So are the excellent large-scale (1:50,000) maps of the Italian Touring Club, which are today quite the best for use in the region. Details of the maps are relegated to the Bibliography.

Naturally, Bolzano of today is dedicated in part to *il turismo*, and the greater one's wish to get away from it all to sleep on a few stones in the middle of nowhere, the more useful it is to acquire a sound working knowledge of the efficient and comprehensive express exits by road and rail. The town is the most convenient starting point for Bressanone and the Val Pusteria; for Merano, the Val Venosta, and Switzerland; for the Brenta; and for Cortina along the Dolomite Road. Around the office of the S.A.D. are seen the coaches that carry passengers in reserved seats, luggage on top either at the same time or in advance; luggage can be left here for those who propose a few days' light travel on foot in the district; the drivers are superb, the conductors helpful, and the services prompt.

The long journey from here through the Val Venosta (Vintschgau) to the Ortler peaks and Switzerland is worth taking on the way to or from Bolzano, and is also covered by the well-known yellow coaches of the Swiss services. The Brenta are farther from here than from Trento, but the journey is again one that is rewarding in itself. It passes over the Mendola (Mendel) road, with wide views over the Adige and the Rosengarten, whilst the Brenta come into sight as soon as the pass is reached. Some hours later the bus climbs up to Campiglio.

But pride of place among bus routes is held unquestioned by that from Bolzano to Cortina by the Dolomite Road. It is one of the most splendid journeys that can be undertaken, and should not be missed. After leaving the outskirts of Bolzano, the route enters the Val d'Ega, through deep narrow gorges of red porphyry, with pines clinging to the sides of the ravines and little sunlight penetrating to the road or the rushing stream alongside. After a few miles the road climbs steadily out of this valley to more open country around Nova Levante (Welschnofen) and shortly afterwards to the woods around Carezza al Lago (Karersee), where the shallow green lake reflects the spires of the Latemar, and over the tree-tops to the north are the southern walls of the Rosengarten. These are the first Dolomites to be seen closely, yet are little more than a formal introduction to the mountains (Plates 17 and 18). The best is yet to be. The Passo di Costalunga (Karer Pass) is the high gateway to the upper Val di Fassa, a fine side entrance at the right point, for the lower valley is less remarkable in its scenery. Hereabouts, they say, is the crater of an ancient volcano, the edges of which are the granitic crags which guard the higher Dolomite. The upper part of the valley ends in the low, grassy Pordoi Pass through which the road climbs with many well-engineered curves, to descend in a similar tortuous way to Livinallongo (Buchenstein) and eventually escape over the Falzarego Pass to Cortina.

The valley is broad and fertile, and something of the music and charm of Italy is in even the string of village names that lie between the Costalunga descent and the Pordoi: Vigo, Pozza, Pera, Mazzin, Fontanazzo, Campestrin, Canazei, and Campitello. To an Englishman the disadvantage of such a valley in summer is its heat, and the higher Sella Inn, on the pass, or the Col di Lana Inn at Pordoi, is pleasanter. But these attractive villages each and all deserve a visit. Their campaniled churches, sometimes with outer galleries in Tyrolese style, with pearl-grey wooden cobbles as roofing instead of the pantiles of the Adige, the stuccoed and frescoed houses, the carved galleries, even the hay chalets have that element of grace that the Italians can bring to the simplest forms of domestic architecture. Their setting is superb. Above the wooded hills are glimpses of the Rosengarten near Vigo or Pera, whilst from the upper villages the towering Sasso Lungo and Sella crags can be seen. Along the whole length of the valley the Sasso Pordoi, with its varied tints, its double line of mural crags divided by a white band of scree, is framed by the dark pines of the valley sides. It is a valley to which the artist or photographer could give more than a proper share of free time, if he is to see the inner recesses of the mountains as well, in a short holiday.

The mountains have changed not at all since the days when Gilbert and Churchill wandered into this valley, but the villages have moved on considerably. Admittedly they still lack the house-proud "spit and polish" of the Austrian valleys, but there is little or nothing of the squalor and ignorance remarked by these early explorers, who found Campitello "dirty, disorderly and of shiftless physiognomy like too many of those in Italy". It was here at the inn that they found "the larder was a box on the stairs containing an antiquated tongue or two looking much more like wood than flesh". The inns today are very different, and those travellers who like a good meal, a bath, and a pleasant room are likely to find them in any village of Fassa. Rizzi's Inn at Vigo, mentioned often in the old nineteenth-century travellers' tales has, like many others, been modernised and extended. Yet its ancient tradition is retained in the fresco of St Christopher, patron saint of travellers, on the wall. The crucifix at its side, like the many others along the roads, and the little shrines of every Alpine track are reminders that we are among a simple peasantry of the Catholic faith, in a land that was for a thousand years a part of the Holy Roman Empire.

Beyond Canazei, the last village, the road divides (Plate 29). A sinuous northern branch winds under the steep Pordoi cliffs, over the Sella Pass by the towers at the end of the plateau, to the famous mountain inn of the Albergo Passo Sella (Sellajochhaus). The other branch turns east to Pordoi. From here is a wide-ranging view. Over the Fassa villages is the line of the Rosengarten; the Pordoi slopes are just above the pass (Plate 24); and peeping round the corner, looking a mere half-mile away in the clear air of a fine day, are the Cinque Dita (Fünffingerspitze) and Punta Grohmann (Plate 25). A few minutes' stroll up the grass slope towards the Sasso Pordoi lifts us above the level of the grassy knolls south of the pass, and the gleaming glacier of the Marmolata breaks the skyline. An excellent walk from Pordoi over these same grassy knolls brings the Marmolata into fuller view, and an easy descent can be made to the Fedaia inns.

To the east the view is even more open. The Tofane and the Falzarego Pass above Cortina are level with our pass, and below the numberless hairpin bends is Arabba, the village of Livinallongo, with a branch road to Caprile. At Arabba the Civetta profile dominates the whole glen (Plate 26).

A few kilometres past Arabba the road turns north, following the contours, twisting among the pines to make height in the two-thousand-foot rise to Falzarego: past the ruined castle of Andraz on its crag, past the pointed Sasso di Stria, and under a long line of south-facing cliffs that culminate in the tremendous walls of the Tofana, little more than half a mile from the road. This line of dolomite rock is in full view for several miles, and though foreshortened since we are so much below its level, is none the less one of the most impressive sights the road can provide (Plate 68). To the south are the lesser summits, the Cinque Torri, the Nuvolau, and the spires of the Croda da Lago.

Soon after the Tofane are passed, the last descent to Cortina begins at Pocol, where the road is engineered around the steep promontory of Crepa and sweeps down the last hillside in long curves. Below, spread out like a map, is the Ampezzo valley, with the white buildings and the campanile of Cortina standing out from the green meadows (Plate 28).

Cortina is a town on the Swiss model. That is to say, it has a few ancient glories, as Brigue perhaps has its Château Stockalper, but mainly it is the creation of a mountaineering age. The crests of the old families of the commune are still seen in fading frescoes on the wall of a town building, whilst the elaborate campanile that looks so incongruous among the nearby hovels in old Victorian prints has now settled down more comfortably in the newer surroundings of the modern neon-lit shops, the tall hotels, the bars, the offices of tourism, and other trivialities of a fashionable resort. For Cortina is to the Eastern Dolomites what Grindelwald, Chamonix, or Zermatt are to the Western Alps.

The peaks are different, rock predominating over ice and snow: Cristallo instead of the Wetterhorn or Eiger; Pelmo instead of the Matterhorn; the Croda da Lago, the Cinque Torri, the Cime di Lavaredo, instead of the Aiguilles. But the cafés, the picture postcards, the cable elevators, the select viewpoints are all there. The guides seem to be mostly dashing young peasants who carry through the summer that air of having been lions among the admiring young women whom they taught to ski in the winter; they clank their pitons and *moschetoni*. Photographs of their latest fancy climbs appear in Ghedina's shop or in the offices of tourism.

The true wanderer, whether walker or climber, who loves the quiet of the mountains, will find Cortina little more than a convenient place to leave

. Ortisei, with the Sasso Lungo: Val Gardena (Grödnerthal)
. A Path through the Fields, Val Gardena

WOOD-CARVINGS OF GRÖDEN (GARDENA)

32. The Largest Wood-Carving in Ortisei

33. Steinadler

34. The Rock Clim

35. Shepherd Boy

36. Goose Girl

. Santa Cristina, Val Gardena

38. Ladinian Peasant with Ox-char
39. The Sasso Lungo (Langkofel) from the Suisi (Seiser) Alp

). Ladinians of the Val Gardena in Traditional Costume

41. Morning Sun in the Val Gardena

:he Capanna Vicenza (Langkofelhütte) under the
Iorth-East Wall of the Sasso Piatto (Plattkofel)

:he Forcella di Sasso Lungo (Langkofeljoch), with the
:inque Dita (Fünffingerspitze), from the North

43. Crags of Sasso Piatto, with Monte Sciliar (Schlern) in the distance

45. The Sasso Lungo, Cima Sud (Langkofeleck), from the South

46. The Sella Plateau and Towers from the Forcella di Sasso Lungo
47. Le Odli (Geisler Group with Fermedaturme and Sass Rigais) from the Sella Pass

8. The San Martino Group and, below, the Col Rodella, from the Forcella di Sasso Lungo
9. The Catinaccio and, below, the First Sella Tower, from the Second Tower

50. Selva (Wolkenstein), the Last Village in the Val Gardena

1. The Northern Ramparts of the Sella Plateau from the Passo Gardena (Grödnerjoch)
2. The Val Culea and the Pisciadu Crags from the same point

53. The Val Lasties from the Zalei Alp
54. The Sasso di Pordoi (Pordoispitze)

The Catinaccio (Rosengarten) at Sunrise

56. Dirupi di Larsec
58. The Winkler Tower from Stabeler with the Marmolata in the distance

57. Below the Vajolet Towers
59. The Northern Tower and the Catinacc d'Antermoia (Kesselkogel)

. The Marmolata Group
The Gran Vernel from the Avisio Woods

62. The Ombretta Pass below the Marmolata
63. Early morning: Pelmo and Civetta from the Ombretta Pass

surplus baggage, before putting a mountain ridge between himself and this stylish, overgrown village. Two or three hours' walking will bring him into the ruder and thus more congenial scenery to the north or east.

Yet Cortina is a pleasant enough place to many people who like to look at mountains whilst taking their ease at their inn, and from such well-placed hotels as the Faloria the view of the Tofane alone are worth close study in all their changefulness.

THE NORTHERN APPROACH

Cortina can also be approached from Bolzano by the longer, less direct approach, which is also the best way to reach it from Innsbruck.

From Bolzano the Brenner line goes up the Isarco valley, along the famous Kunter's Weg, where road, rail, and river march together with a few feet to spare between them. Once this gorge is passed Chiusa (Klausen) is reached, with its crowded houses in the valley, its ancient castle Branzoll, and high up on the crag that has been called the Gibraltar of Tyrol, the old Benedictine cloister of Säben (Sabiona), formerly the castle of the Prince Bishops of Brixen (Bressanone) (Plate 15).

Bressanone and Fortezza are soon reached, both beautiful little towns full of old streets and churches. Here we leave the Brenner route to turn east along the wider Val Pusteria (Pusterthal). On this part of the northern approach there is little indication of the imminence of the Dolomites. There are no craggy heralds like the Adige cliffs; the rock is granitic, the hillslopes more gentle, the larches and pines more insistent. There are no vines, and the villages have exclusively what Bolzano and its neighbours had predominantly, the Austro-Tyrolese aspect. Autumn comes early here, for it is a valley that is allied more to its northern neighbours than to the sunny Italian south. I have passed along it in the moonlight of the early hours of an October day, when the haypoles stood up into thin streamers of mist and a hoar frost lay over all, a day when no frost would be known in the southern valleys of the region.

Occasionally, nearing Dobbiaco (Toblach), glimpses of the Dolomite fringe are seen through the side valleys, but the full grandeur of the mountains is not with us until the gateway to the south is passed below Dobbiaco. There the Strada Alemagna runs quickly into the narrow glen towards Landro, the steep cliffs reappear, and the shoulders of the Sexten peaks reach down from the sky. At Landro a dramatic unfolding of the landscape takes place, with the spiky

Cime di Lavaredo (Drei Zinnen) standing at the head of the valley Rienza (Plate 86). A mile further on is the Lago di Landro, with the most spectacular skyline of any lake I have yet seen. It is finer even than the Oeschinensee, and the north faces of Cristallo and Popena are comparable in scenic quality with the best aspects of La Meije or the south side of Mont Blanc (Plate 87).

The latter comparison was originally made by one of the earliest pioneers of the Dolomite Mountains, F. F. Tuckett, who approached by this route from Lienz in 1863, remarking in his diary that he found here at the Dürrensee, as it was then called, "a most glorious peak with a glacier in front . . . the Cristallo struck me as finer than the Géant from Courmayeur".

After Carbonin (Schluderbach), the next village, only a few miles over the easy Ampezzo Pass remain before Cortina is reached. On the west the high and richly tinted Croda Rossa is the dominant peak of the landscape, until just before Cortina the view ahead of Sorapis and the more distant Antelao compels attention.

The road runs through Cortina to San Vito, with its even grander aspects of Antelao and of Pelmo, to Pieve di Cadore, the birthplace of Titian. He was one of the first painters to introduce the colour and wild craggy forms of the Dolomite landscape into his paintings, though he did so mainly in backgrounds to figure groups, for he painted before any appreciation of pure landscape had developed. It is to his knowledge of his native hills of Cadore that much of his command of colour is attributed. Pieve, like all the villages on this Venetian fringe, is completely Italian, for it was never so fully within the Austrian sphere of influence as the north-west, although nominally part of the Empire from the time of the Venetian collapse until 1866.

Of great mercantile significance was this eastern road in reverse, the approach to Austria from Venice and Belluno, by the Piave valley to Cadore and Cortina, over the Ampezzo Pass and down to Dobbiaco (Toblach) and the Val Pusteria (Pusterthal). It was the road of the Venetian traders, and passed mainly through their own territory on the mainland. For some reason it was known from the north as the Heidenstrasse, the "heathens' road"; but from the south it was, as it is today, the Strada Alemagna.

The South Tyrol Problem

THE Dolomite region is the old Süd Tirol of the Austro-Hungarian Empire, and though the name is banished from all official maps of modern Italy, it is only since 1919 that the region has been Italian. Just what validity there is in the claims made both by Austria and Italy from time to time, and still likely to be renewed by the former, is in itself an interesting study.

The early divisions of the region were those of the Prince Bishoprics of Brixen and of Trent, both part of the Holy Roman Empire. The latter See in particular, although founded in the fifth century, and at that time looking to Rome, was thus by 1027 part of the Germanic succession. In both cases the Bishops, following contemporary custom, or rather necessity, selected as "protector" the Count of Tirol (Teriolis, an old Roman outpost). His castle was Schloss Tirol above Merano, some twenty miles north-west of Bolzano and on the Adige. Eventually the county by inheritance passed to the Habsburgs. From 1363 until 1919 the district was Austrian, in spite of a southern fringe of Italian-speaking towns, including Trento, and this fact is not without significance today, when the South Tyrol question is still unsolved in a way that gives satisfaction to all its inhabitants.

The inhabitants of South Tyrol are as much a racial mixture as the English, and for a similar reason; successive waves of invaders. Three divisions can be seen: Ladinian; Germanic; Italian. The small Ladinian communities probably form the oldest colonists and include many dark-haired Alpine types. Their dialect is Ladin, which is also found in enclaves of the Swiss Alps, being there known as Romansch. These dialects spring from the common Romance stock of Latin just as Spanish and French do, but they have failed to keep pace, have little or no literature, and, like Gaelic and similar survivals, derive their written material from the researches and invention of relatively modern scholarship. The most obviously Ladin valley is that of Gröden, the present Val Gardena, with the valley of Gader (Ladinia) which runs south from Brunico, Livinallongo (Buchenstein), and smaller communities of the Cortina area in the east and the upper Val Fassa in the west.

These definite Ladinian communities are Austro-Tyrolese in sympathy as far as an outsider can judge. Whilst there is no doubt that all the more northern valleys are Austro-Tyrolese in both race and feeling, south of the Ladin areas the reverse applies. The Adige below Bolzano, the Val di Fassa, and points south of Cortina are clearly Italian. There has apparently been considerable ebb and flow of German-Italian peoples over the centuries that passed after Rome and before the rise of modern Italy, for in the seventeenth century a visitor describes Trento as then predominantly German, and there were other communities beyond the Val Sugana. On the other hand, there was much Italian penetration in later years. In some nineteenth-century maps a general title to the Trentine and Venetian parts of the Austrian Empire is "Welsch" Tyrol.

If one were to seek the real division it is not difficult to trace approximately. A line taken from the Tonale Pass, on the western boundary of the Trentino, to the Mendel Pass near Bolzano, then across country eastwards through the massifs of the Rosengarten, Langkofel, Sella, Tofanas, Cristallo, Cime di Lavaredo to the Comelico Pass, would be as close as possible to the ethnographic facts. But simple justice to peasant peoples is necessarily subordinated to matters of state, including demands of military strategy, and to economic factors (such as water power in the Adige). Decision is bedevilled by a hundred other complexities considered by experts in conference chambers. And lastly, in the world as it still is, the winners of any war can claim their spoils.

There is little evidence that the South Tyrol problem was a problem at all until the rise of national feeling for a united Italy, backed by the rather aggressive outlook that a newfound patriotism invariably engenders. Italy came into being as a result of hard struggles, and after the campaigns of 1866, which resulted in the acquisition of Venezia, only the Trentino remained south of the Alps, a strategic menace and an affront to Italian patriots who regarded all Teutons as tyrants.

Straws here and there showed how the feeling was in the nineteenth century. D. W. Freshfield, an early traveller in the Brenta, records seeing a fresco of the life of Mary Magdalene, where the saint before her conversion was shown in a group of men pictured as Austrian officers in full uniform! In one year the good people of Paneveggio in the San Martino Dolomites sang Garibaldi's hymn in honour of the Emperor's birthday. For fifty years such trivial incidents were a symbol and a sign of Italian feeling under Austrian rule.

Later in the century we see another indication of feeling as it was among intellectuals. Vittorio Sella, the great mountaineer and photographer, nephew of the famous Quintino Sella, also a mountaineer and comrade of Garibaldi, visited the Dolomites to take photographs. But nothing is recorded of any visits here *beyond* the Italian frontier—that is, the Marmolata summit ridge, or the Cime de Lavaredo and the Pala peaks, all either fully Italian or on the frontier. His lifelong distaste for the German language is also on record.

* * * *

The rulers of Italy in the Great War prudently remained neutral, whilst bargaining with both sides for the Trentino. The Italian claim on Austria was for a new frontier north of the Nonsberg to Gargazone between Merano and Bolzano, then to Chiusa (Klausen) on the Isarco (Eisack) south of the Val Gardena (Grödnerthal), across to the southern fringe of the Tofane at Falzarego, then upwards to include the Ampezzo valley and Cortina within Italy. This was identical with the old Bishopric of Trent and with the boundary made by Napoleon in 1810 as the kingdom of Italy. The counter-offer by Austria was a refusal to give up either the Val di Fassa or the Cortina districts. This political huckstering broke down because of the strategic issues implicit in either frontier. Eventually Italy secured from the Allies a promise of the fulfilment of the *popular* Italian claim—the watershed of all rivers flowing to the Adriatic; and despite their dubious value as Allies, and in breach of the later principles of self-determination so piously expressed by the victors, this promise was honoured.

The old Austrian frontier fully satisfied no one, and the same criticism applied to the post-Great-War Italian frontier. Moreover, as always, the common man escapes one tyranny only to find another. The rise of aggressive Fascism in Italy meant a policy of Italianisation in the Dolomite district, in education and in administration. The value of the upper Adige to Italian economy became considerable, for the development of water power alone supplied the cities of Lombardy and Venezia. It is a factor not operative in pre-war days, when lack of control of the watershed made such schemes impossible, even had the time been ripe.

After the incorporation of Austria into the Reich, the Hitler–Mussolini alliance made an attempt at solution of the problem of the frontier peoples. Continuance of the anti-Germanic policy being impolitic, and the presence of large German-speaking enclaves a danger to Italy in the new conditions, arrangements were made for a wholesale transfer of populations into the North Tyrol. Part of this transfer had been made before the entry of Italy into the late war, when the Nazi "occupation" of the Trentino began. It may be doubted if they would ever have left had Hitler won the war. But with the collapse of Fascism the area again became one of danger to both sides. The southern fringe of the Dolomites became an outpost of the *partisani*, as Bill Tilman tells us in his vigorous story of his adventures as a liaison officer with them in the region of Belluno, around the San Martino peaks and Agordo.*

Following the collapse of Italy, there was an immediate revival of Austro-Tyrolese feeling in the Bolzano district and points north. The old German signs, which had reappeared with the occupation, were retained, a German language press is operating, and Tyrolese "irredentism" finds expression in demand for self-government, for independence from Italy at least. The Italian efforts to meet this demand—just as popular and fundamental after all as the spirit that surged in the followers of Andreas Hofer when he fought Napoleon the tyrant, or of Garibaldi when he fought for *Italia Irredenta*—have been to allay separatism by granting some regional autonomy, and the creation of a province "Bozen" out of the northern Trentino. Yet the weight of Italian sentiment in the Trentino is allowed preponderance over the smaller weight of Tyrolese feeling in the north. The situation in some ways resembles the pressure being exercised by the southern Irish upon the Ulster community, but with the important difference that Ulster is free from the disadvantages which simple majority rule would impose upon it, as in the Trentino.

A weak Austria is in no position to press claims which might find acceptance if any regard to justice were being had. But at least the South Tyrol in its present condition has a greater freedom than under Mussolini, and that is a major point in practical living for its peoples. Let us hope that by now the Italians have learned that tolerance of local peculiarities is political wisdom, and that if they continue to control they will do so with a mellow detachment that finds nothing objectionable in a German text on a gravestone, or a Tyrolese patriot singing *Zu Mantua im Banden.*

* *When Men and Mountains Meet,* H. W. Tilman, D.S.O., M.C.

War in the Dolomites

THE struggles by the Italians to unite the whole of Italy up to the watershed began in 1848, and the Dolomites have seen three wars in the following century. First, the brief campaign of 1866, when Austria, after a defeat by the Prussians at Königgratz, asked for an armistice after little more than skirmishing had taken place on the Italian front; second, the Great War period, when there was a terrific struggle in many Dolomite areas; third, the last war, when there was little warfare except on the southern and western fringes of the region.

It has been said that in popular estimation the importance of mountains in warfare has been exaggerated and that they play as a rule but a secondary part and that a preliminary one. The decisive battles of history, as many strategists have pointed out, are fought in the plains.

Nevertheless, part of great campaigns have been fought in the mountains, and the Alps as a whole have seen many great captains, from Hannibal to Napoleon and Suvarov. But the most thrilling stories of war in the mountains come from what are perhaps the "sideshows" of campaigns. Andreas Hofer, the patriot of Tyrol, used his men against vastly greater numbers of trained infantry in the mountain gorges, where stone avalanches could wreck half an army. The "sporting" aspects of the Indian North-West Frontier skirmishes are another case where hillmen can do well against well-armed troops.

In the Dolomites, a frontier region of three modern wars, there were many encounters which make good reading, and which reveal fighting men in terrain where the individual matters and the small group is the effective unit.

In 1866 the Italo-Austrian War was being fought, and an Austrian officer,

Julius Meurer, many years later visited the Alpine Club in London, of which he was a member, and gave a striking account of a small skirmish among these hills which still conveys a vivid impression:

> "...Above Auronzo were encamped five companies of Austrian chasseurs (Alpenjäger) stretched on the wet, dew-besprinkled grass.... In the midst of the group stood the officers and held a council of war; on a rock lay, spread before them, the map, which was examined by the pale light of a burning pine torch. I was among this group of officers. Only with the effort of my whole energy was I able to keep off sleep, for it had been my bad luck to spend the night between two night marches as the commanding officer of the outposts.
>
> "Through the dense mist in the east gleamed sometimes the reddish, faint, trembling light of the young day, and the figures near stood out plainly and more plainly. Then suddenly, touched as it were by a fairy wand, the mist broke asunder and hid itself in the valleys.... Farther in the west rose from the vanishing realm of haze the proud pinnacles of the Ampezzo Dolomites, the beautiful, the magic promised land, at that time still adorned with the virgin wreath.... At the sight of the rising sun the men, touched as it were by an electric shock, jumped up, for they were all sons of the mountain whose hearts beat quicker at the sight of this fairy-like glorious vision. With new vigour the march into the valley was begun. It became evident at some distance from Auronzo that the place had at our approach been evacuated by the Garibaldians. Our first care was to procure rest, food, and drink. Scarcely two short hours had I enjoyed sweet sleep when I heard the alarm call of the shrill bugle horn, and in a few minutes I stood at the rallying point of my company.
>
> "There indeed took place a skirmish which an Alpine climber as a spectator would have witnessed with special pleasure. Not intrepidity and valour alone, but also dexterity, boldness, and skill in climbing were auxiliaries to our success. With cat-like skill, our brave chasseurs climbed from position to position to fall upon the enemy sideways, and the Garibaldians, to prevent our doing this, also mounted higher and higher, keeping pace with us. In a short time the mountain glen was right and left up to the top one single chain of fire. Grave and dumb, the pale yellow, venerable Dolomite summits looked down astonished on these wild proceedings. From their iron walls, which had braved centuries, the sound of

> the crackling volleys and the lengthened signals of the bugle horns re-echoed a hundredfold in the mountains. In this Alpine war we spent a part of August 14th."

Such was battle in the 'sixties.

* * * *

The 1915 war, when Italy joined the Allies, was marked by instant action along the whole Dolomite frontier. The Alpini and Alpenjäger regiments, with light mountain artillery regiments in support, performed magnificent feats of mountaineering among these appalling peaks. Tunnels and caves were carved in the ice of the Marmolata glacier. Light guns were established in the most exposed and elevated sites, whilst on the plateaux in particular very extensive tunnelling was done, and the lines go over ridges and to such summits as that of the Paternkofel, the Tofane, and the Marmolata. Many of the fortifications are still in existence, for instance the tunnels of the Sexten area, and on the Col Ombretta in 1947 were the remains of machine-gun posts and even fragments of barbed wire, which certainly are not of the recent war.

The splendid tenacity of both sides indicates the fundamental stamina of the mountain people whether Italian or Austrian. Italian patrols made the first ascent of the south face of the Marmolata di Rocca, whilst the old South Wall route (Plates 145 to 149) was descended for the first time. Among the more fantastic achievements of mining, the top was blown off a Cortina peak. Monte Grappa, south of the Primiero valley, was heavily equipped with artillery emplacements, and considerable fighting took place all along the valley from the Rolle Pass, through San Martino which was destroyed, Primiero which fortunately survived, to Fonsazo at the fringe of the mountains.

Further west the Sugana line was held, and the Italians never occupied Trento until after the armistice, being content to occupy the towns between it and Verona. This was, of course, in country negotiable by the ordinary infantry, and so that area of battle is outside the region where the Alpini so distinguished themselves.

The aftermath of the Great War, once the first great upheaval of the change from Austrian to Italian control was over, saw one of the most remarkable monuments created to the memory of these fierce struggles in the peaks. On a hill to the west of Cortina is set a massive granite campanile, the memorial to the finest troops in Europe, the Alpini of Italy and the Alpenjäger of Austria, who for three years fought each other with gallantry on this Dolomite front.

The memorial would be a striking cenotaph to either side, but as a monument to *both* is more strange and moving than can be imagined. The panels of names, now Austrian, now Italian, alternate around the inner hall, in the centre of which is a tomb to the Italian general who died with his men. The tower looks to many scenes of their battles, the Tofane, and beyond the Tre Croci Pass. Below are the farms and cottages that bred many of those whose bones are in the tombs of the monument. It is not difficult to sense the tragedy of such a district as this where, in the war between Latin and Teuton, friends and neighbours of peace had to divide into what can have differed little from the agony of a civil war.

Mountain Names

In every mountain district the advent of military surveyors has brought up the difficulty of names, for where only a peasant population has been living many mountains have no name; yet others are differently named according to their aspect from opposite valleys; and when there is a language frontier as in the Dolomites, added confusion can arise. The enigma of Stac Polly in Wester Ross has many counterparts in the South Tyrol.

But the principal difficulty in the frontier regions of the Dolomites has been the wholesale change-over since 1919. As a result it is not easy to follow the older literature from present-day guides or maps. A list of the most important changes is given in the Glossary, to help those readers who have ready to hand a modern map when looking at original accounts by the old explorers.

Some changes are straightforward translations. Sasso Lungo and Cinque Dita are obviously deduced from Langkofel and Fünffingerspitze, and perhaps have the virtue of being more euphonious to English ears. The advantage is not entirely with Italian, however. The loss of the pleasant legendary name of Rosengarten in favour of Catinaccio is difficult to accept, though an effort to retain the legend is seen in the change from Laurinswand to Croda del Rey Laurino. But that association with the devil, Der Teufelswand, south of the Rosengarten, has disappeared.

The Primiero peaks and those around the Marmolata have mainly been retained unaltered, for they always were Italian. Similarly with the Cortina d'Ampezzo and Auronzo groups, except certain small peaks or towers. But the fringe of the Sexten district is radically changed. Admittedly the translation to Cima Undici and Dodici is literal for Elferkofel and Zwölferkofel, although the principal name of the latter peak was formerly understood to be Col Agnello, and it is so named in older records. But the peaks named Elfer, Zwölfer, and Einser are pre-eminently correct from Sexten, since they are respectively below the sun at the hours mentioned. Cima Dodici in particular suggests another (and more usual) derivation from Dodici Apostoli, which is often found in Italy, where St Luke, St Mark, St Matthew, the Madonna, and other sacred names of the New Testament all have their ridges, turrets, campaniles, woods, and villages, such as the Pale di San Lucano, the Cima della Madonna, the Bosco di San Marco, the village of San Matteo.

On the other hand, the naming of the Drei Zinnen as the Tre Cime di Lavaredo is no more than a restoration of an equally old name, and even from the northern side a century ago the pass to the east of these peaks was known as the Lavaredo Sattel. Dr Grohmann was criticised for calling it the Paternsattel, as well as for many other Germanisations, by Sir Maurice Holzmann, a contemporary authority. The Germanisation in the details of the Rosengarten by Merzbacher was similarly commented upon.

To some extent it seems that in the early years of survey and exploration the Austrian engineers and climbers were only retorting to the "irredentist" movement in stressing or adopting names in their own tongue. Occasionally they risked appearing rather ridiculous by too obviously departing from established titles. To christen the Cima di Brenta the Kaiser-Franz-Josef-Spitze was going too far. But one name at least was wholly appropriate, the Guglia di Brenta, named by the Austrians. The modern Italian guide-book to the district is unnecessarily crisp about this—"a Germanic climber, one Schultz, quite arbitrarily chose the name of Guglia di Brenta, introducing the term Guglia unknown in the whole of the Trentino". But this name for the pinnacle is at least distinctive and worthy of its unique outline, whilst its official name of Campanile Basso leaves it nominally inferior to the Campanile Alto, a good though much less spire-like summit. Very few of the other Brenta names were altered, for they were standardised between the differing claims of the Val Rendena and the Molveno valley by the Societa degli Alpinisti Tridentini from 1874 onwards, before which (for instance) the Brenta Alta had, from the east, been the name of the Cima Tosa, and many other points of confusion had existed.

Walking Tours

A GOOD climbing district is not always well adapted for walking, particularly for walking tours. In the Alps, for instance, though there are many delightful walks in any valley, the pedestrian tourist pure and simple is too often hemmed in by glacier or rock walls which are impassable. Moreover, the large scale of the valleys and the extent to which the steep lower cliffs impend mean that there is a restricted expanse of mountain scenery visible from low levels, and even that changes its aspect only gradually. To take one example only, a walk up the long valley from Stalden to Zermatt is certainly pleasant in its close-range views of roaring torrent and steep woodland, but of the great peaks only rare glimpses are obtained for the greater part of twenty miles. At Zermatt a crossing to either of the lateral valleys of Saas or Zinal or southwards into Italy is barred by glacier passes which lie beyond the capacities and skill of the strongest walker who is not a trained mountaineer, unless he is prepared to engage a guide or can join a rope of Alpinists.

The Dolomites, on the other hand, are perfectly adapted for the cross-country walker. Not only can splendid head-to-foot views of many peaks be secured from valley levels (*e.g.* at Cortina) but also the passes are almost entirely snow-free, whilst the smaller scale of the valleys themselves makes for frequent changes of scene in the course of a day's march.

Here in England and in many parts of the Continent there are chains of Youth Hostels arranged to allow a good day's walk in mountain country when passing from one to another. The comfortable mountain inns of the Dolomites, similar to those in the North Tyrol, are adapted to many more types of walker than Youth Hostels where cheapness is the main object. These inns vary somewhat in the amenities they offer, according to situation, but follow a fairly settled plan. Dormitories with six or eight bunks are available on very cheap terms, and walkers may bring their own food. The same *rifugio* will also provide private bedrooms, often with a comfortable sheet-lined bed, and a full bill of fare, for the man who prefers a higher level of comfort. Needless to say, the cuisine is of high standard, whilst good wines are never lacking. Those who are fond of solitude will perhaps complain that the inns are met rather too frequently, but a careful choice of route will enable some of them to be avoided.

Anyone who is capable of dealing with the rough walking met in Skye, in Wester Ross, on Tryfan and the Glyders, on Striding Edge or the "traverse" of Great Gable, will be capable of proceeding along Dolomite tracks. Tourists, as Baedeker has it, "should have steady heads", for often the tracks pass along precipices and zigzag up steep slopes. But the German and Austrian Alpine Club, in making many routes widely accessible, did so thoroughly, and though iron stanchions, wire ropes, and ladders are out of place on a good rock climb, they do little harm when used to assist the approach to a hut, or where an intricate and potentially dangerous track weaves its way among precipices. Even so, the majority of tracks are not decorated in this way at all—the ladders or chains are the exceptions. The waymarks are less open to general criticism. The inability of novices to find their way except by following splashes of paint on trees or rocks has often been criticised. But though the scale of the Dolomites is small by Swiss standards, it is large to those who come from flatter lands, and, especially in the wooded slopes, a marked track is a help. Those who prefer to go by map and compass may do so, but at intermediate levels no particular merit is acquired and much time can be lost. Among the crags, absence of clear routes would spell unjustifiable danger for walkers in bad weather.

Walking with a full rucksack, as one inevitably needs to do on a tour, is warm work anywhere, and Italy is hot. The best time for walking is in late summer or early autumn, even at the risk of finding some huts closed. Similarly, those who prefer to see at least some snow on their hills may prefer the spring, a time of particular beauty. Again the huts may not all be open, and enquiry should be made before leaving a valley centre. In general, early June to mid-September is the time when *all* huts will be available. Valley walking pure and simple is apt to be oppressive, and a high-level tour is much better. By keeping to the 5–8,000-foot contours, where the fringe of the tree-line, on the one hand, and the average base-level of the difficult rock, on the other hand, form the boundaries, the traveller is rewarded by open views, yet views whose starkness is relieved at times by woodland and green alp. A worthwhile compromise between the restricted valley walking from an hotel and the overladen tour is to make a way to a hut and do two or three days' walking from that base before returning to the valley.

Main roads are emphatically not recommended, and not merely because, like main roads anywhere, they are hard to walk on, but also because being constructed of limestone and churned up by heavy motor transport they are covered in fine dust. The clouds sent up by every wheel not only create discomfort for those near, but also overlay the boundary grass and trees with a grey film, just as if they were near a cement works. Fortunately the roads can easily be avoided, except for an occasional direct crossing. In general the area is made accessible at selected points by these roads, and their separation is great enough to leave between them large areas of mountain country. Even where a road goes eventually to the walker's destination, alternatives exist in woodland tracks at a satisfactory distance from the highway.

One of the delightful features of walking in the Dolomite grasslands and woods is the wealth of flowers. I am no botanist, and cannot attempt to impress my readers with long strings of names, but from a mass of impressions it is easy to recall the grass slopes of the Sella Pass in July, with gentians almost as numerous as the grass blades; the tiny summit of a bleak, bony pinnacle in the Rosengarten with a clump of Alpine buttercups growing in a sheltered crevice; the cushion mosses and clusters of soldanella on an almost vertical face of rock in the San Martino Dolomites; the lilac-tinted autumn crocus dotted over the parklands behind Castel Pietra on an October day; the massed clumps of alpenrose among the boulders of the Val Brenta on a day of mist and storm.

Though everywhere the walking routes alone justify a visit by small energetic parties of the moderate amount of mountain experience I have mentioned, there is no doubt that the party able to get the best out of a Dolomite tour is one whose members have some experience of mountaineering and rock-climbing. The scale of the hills is such that by starting early from a hut an easy peak can be reached in three or four hours, descended in half the time, and the walk continued to another hut.

Mountain wanderings of this kind, mixing walking with a little climbing, are perhaps the finest holiday possible. They appeal especially to the artist or the photographer, neither of whom cares to be tied to a rigid time-table, which might compel him to abandon a promising landscape in changing weather because of the insistent pressure of the flying minutes that a Swiss glacier and mountain tour involves. Scenically, the absence of clean snowfields is sometimes to be regretted, but beautiful as snow can be, it can also be appallingly oppressive to wade through leagues of it, softened in the hot sun when the climber "feels himself spent and fumbles for his brains". The dazzling Dolomite scree can at least be walked over without the need to rope the party and maintain the unrelenting vigilance among crevasses that can prevent the free enjoyment of scenery in the Swiss highlands.

By comparison with Britain, where similar divisions of the day between rock-climbing and walking can be made, the Dolomites seem a fulfilment of what so often is a mere promise of good climbing. It has been said of our shorter rock routes that they end just when they are beginning to be interesting. The longer Dolomite routes thus offer more solid satisfaction.

Exploration of these mountains has long since ended, in the official sense, yet is it not open to everyone to make his own personal discoveries? He may be confident that in the great variety of walks and scrambles available, and set out on the maps of the district, he will be able to measure the risks against his own experience, and by suitable selection and gradual experiment avoid finding himself involved in such dangerous positions as the Alps can bring, yet with considerably more exhilarating situations and more massive rock architecture than are found in Britain.

Moreover, the merely dull weather, such as we have all too often at home in the mountains, is rare. The continental climate means many brilliant days of sun, with perhaps fine-weather mists drifting along the crags at noon; or a brief afternoon storm, clearing again as the cooler evening air disperses the clouds. When the storms do break, they *are* storms, with hail and thunder, lightning, and all the drama that might be expected. But the clearance of the storm can again bring unthought-of grandeur to the rock pinnacles as one summit after another is revealed in the boiling mists, "splendid as an army with banners", and gleaming with fresh snow.

To the general tourists and solitary mountain wanderers I recommend only those ascents that to the climber are "easy" peaks. They exist in every district. The Sciliar, Piz Cir, or Sasso Piatto near Gardena; the Vezzana or the Rosetta at San Martino; the Tofanas, the Nuvolau, the Punta Nera, and many others at Cortina; the Brenta Bassa and the Cima Brenta above Campiglio—most are graded I or II, and so perfectly suitable for the steady guideless party of some experience and the ability to read a German or Italian guidebook and trace a well-worn mountaineering route up or down.

. Cortina, with Monte Cristallo and the Tre Croci Pass

. The Ridge of Pomagagnon

66. Punta Nera of Sorapis
67. West Ridges of Sorapis from Faloria

8. The South Wall of Tofana di Rozes with the Torre Inglese in the right foreground

69. Evening Light: Cristallo and Piz Popena from near Tre Croci

›. La Cesta of Sorapis

71. Monte Piano at Sunrise, from Misurina
72. The Tre Cime di Lavaredo (Drei Zinnen) from Misurina

. The Valley leading to Auronzo, from below the Cime di Lavaredo

74. The Cadini Group from the Caldart Hut
75. Clearing Storms: Cima Dodici (Zwölferkofel)

6. Morning Sun : Cima Undici (Elferkofel)
7. Evening Sun: the Forcella di Giralba

78. Cima Dodici (Zwölferkofel) from the North

9. The Cime di Lavaredo (Drei Zinnen) from the North
0. The Cima Una and Crode Fiscaline (Einserkofel and Oberbachernspitzen)

81. The Punta di Tre Scarperi from San Candido (Innichen)
82. Evening in the Val Pusteria from Dobbiaco (Toblach)

The Punta di Tre Scarperi (Dreischusterspitze) from the South

84. The Val Rinbon, and the Beginning of the Valle di Rinbianco at the top

. Val Rinbon with Monte Piano and the Croda Rossa (Hohe Gaisl)
. Looking back to the Cime di Lavaredo from near Landro

87. The Lago di Landro (Dürrensee)

Dolomite rock-climbing proper is a very different matter. Here the art has been as highly elaborated as in any other rock-climbing district. The ascents compare in difficulty with the best that Britain, the Chamonix Aiguilles, or the Bavarian highlands can show.

But it is in the wide field of advanced rock-climbing that much of the present-day appeal of these mountains lies, and so fuller consideration of it is deferred to a special chapter at the end of the book.

Groups of Peaks and Valleys

THE sections of the book which follow are mere introductions, necessarily brief and based upon personal experiences, to the various groups.

VALLEY	GROUPS OF PEAKS NEARBY	
	Italian Name	*German Name*
The Val Gardena	Sciliar	Schlern
(*Grödnerthal*)	Sasso Lungo	Langkofel
	Sella	Sella
	Cir	Tschierspitzen
	Odli	Geislergruppe
The Val di Fassa	Catinaccio	Rosengarten
	Marmolada	Marmolata
The Val d'Ampezzo	Ampezzo	Ampezzo
	Val Sesto	Sexten
	Auronzo	Auronzo
The Val Cismon	San Martino	San Martino
	Primiero	Primiero
The Val Campiglio	Gruppo di Brenta	Brentagruppe

THE VAL GARDENA

The Val Gardena is hidden away beyond the Sasso Lungo (Langkofel) and Sciliar (Schlern) from the south, or the Odli (Geisler) group from the north. Its outlet, high above the Isarco (Eisack), is not easily seen; and it is not difficult to understand why it has retained a distinctive character from early times. It is the principal Ladinian valley, and these small, dark "Alpine" people are as different from the stolid Teutons of the Pusterthal as from the even more

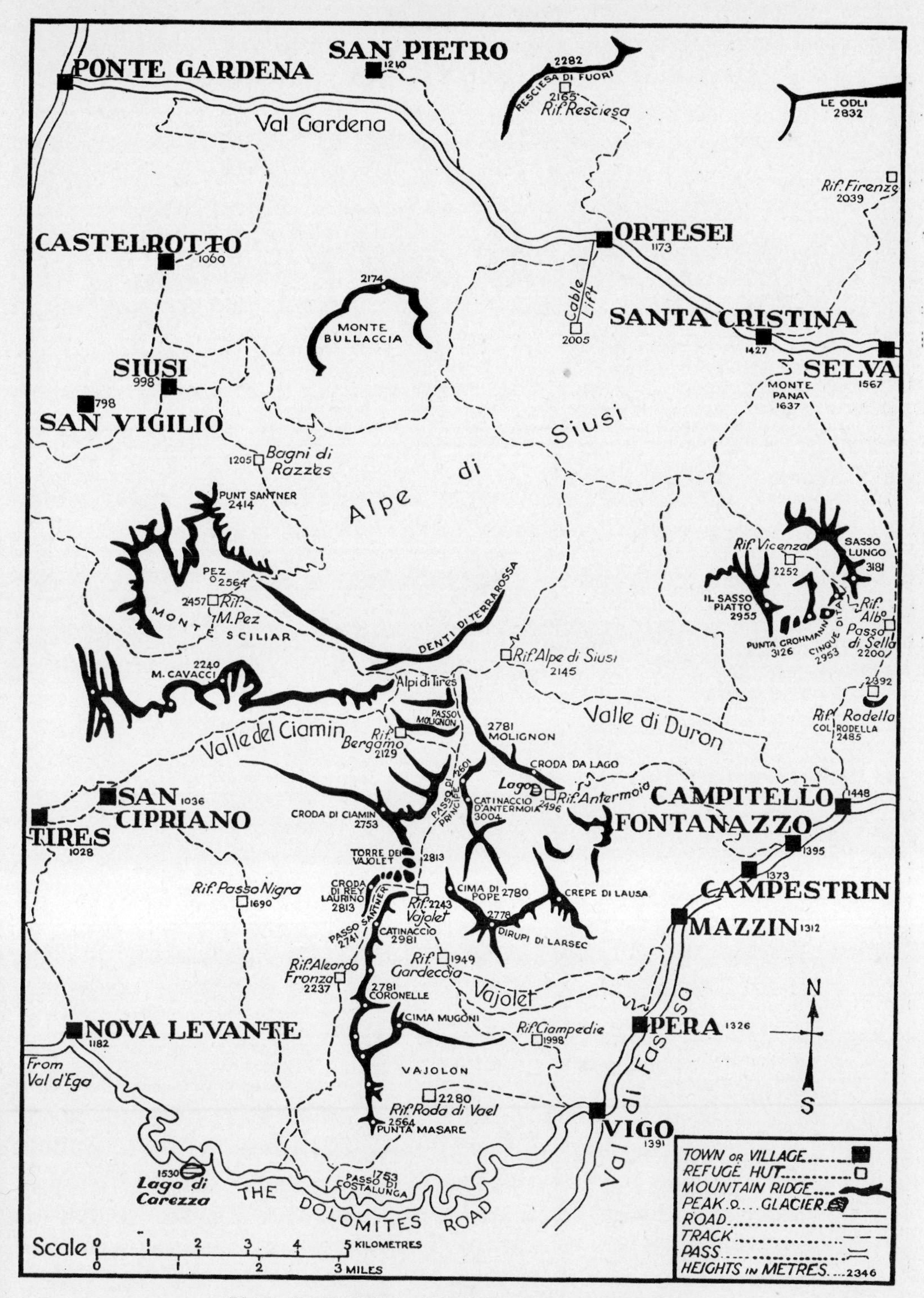

VAL GARDENA–CATINACCIO GROUPS

vivacious Italianate inhabitants of the Fassa valley immediately to the south, beyond the Sasso Lungo.

I think the Gröden valley is the most southerly one which has a Tyrolese type of costume. Naturally this is only for *les dimanches et les jours de fête*, and is not worn for everyday work. The costumes are very colourful and ornate. The men's dress is an interesting change from the standardised leather shorts that are part of the accepted costume of the North Tyrol. They wear black flowered velvet waistcoats, white shirts with coloured cravats, black knee breeches and, inevitably, the white stockings that are always seen throughout the Austrian lands. Some have scarlet braces, of the usual Tyrolese type, and important accessories like the cummerbund belts, richly embroidered. Hats again are variable, many men wearing the broad green hat, others wear smaller black hats (Plate 40).

The women's dresses vary considerably in detail but follow a general scheme of richly embroidered bodices and aprons over white lace blouses, whilst their hats are wide-brimmed, of olive-green silk and felt. Those women who do not wear the large hats sometimes have gilt coronets or other similar headgear (possibly mainly used for the Corpus Christi festival).

* * * *

The valley is easily entered by road from the Ponte all'Isarco, or by rail from Chiusa, whence the little mountain railway winds up the long hillside in steep curves, but the finest approach is by Castelrotto. Above this village begins the vast Alp, the largest stretch of woodland and pasture in the region, the Alpe di Siusi. Bounded on the south by the slopes of the Sciliar and the fantastic crags of the Sasso Lungo group, it stretches east almost to the Sella plateau. The Alp is a rolling plateau about twelve miles long and up to eight miles broad. It is high enough to give invigorating air, and it is not necessary to walk its length or even its breadth to find good food and lodging. The alternation of pasture with pine woods with the constant background of the peaks themselves makes a fascinating introduction to the Dolomites. By keeping to the northern side of the Alp, we can at any point descend into the Gardena valley, perhaps above Ortisei, formerly St Ulrich, the principal village and a popular Italian resort. Clean, neat, colourful, it has more elegance and artistry in its streets than half the villages of Switzerland. The alternation of Tyrolese carved balconies in natural pine with the tinted stucco of the more modern buildings leaves an impression of the happy blending of two civilisations.

It is hereabouts that the long-established wood-carving industry is carried on. The old Austrian State School of Woodcarving has been continued since the valley became Italian, and the quality of the work surpasses that of either Bavaria or Switzerland. It was a journeyman woodcarver named Johann Demetz who is credited with the wide repute of the products of the valley, and there is still at least one Demetz family in Santa Cristina, a charming village two miles above Ortisei. But the present Johann is a guide and a good one. He is pictured on the photographs here and there, and is well known among English climbers, though he speaks barely a word of our language. Calling himself at times Giovanni de Mez (for Italianisation is perhaps good business), he prefers to speak Tyrolese-German rather than Italian. His elder son, who also is to be a guide some day, carved the climber which is reproduced on Plate 34. It was an early creation to represent his father, and I think he was delighted to make it his first sale.

There is, of course, a considerable amount of work done by these peasant carvers at home in winter, which might be called "bread and butter" work. Such standard articles as the old Gemsjäger, bearded, in shorts, with his flintlock at the ready, find their counterpart in North Tyrol and Bavaria, as do the Steinadler and Steinbock. A good many slighter models of animals, for use as toys, are also seen. But the really beautiful work of the valley is seen in such small groups as the shepherd boy and goose-girl of Plates 35 and 36, and in the crucifixes and other sacred images for which naturally there is a wide demand throughout the Catholic world. Perhaps the largest carving produced by the valley is that of the Roman soldier in the high street of Ortisei, whose spear reaches beyond the fourth story of the adjacent inn (Plate 32).

But carving is only one occupation added to agriculture. If the Adige valley around Bolzano is famed for its fruit and vines, the Gardena valley is equally known for its dairy products. The great Alp, feeding cattle in summer and providing much winter fodder, is the mainstay of the whole valley, and the prosperous farms are to be seen everywhere, with their *sennhütten* dependencies high above them beyond the steep forested flanks of the valley.

The difficulties of making any sort of track through the forests and the steepness of the ground mean that the peasant carts, or chars, are much smaller and narrower than in flatter lands. Thus they are suited to the narrow cuttings and to the smaller loads than can be pulled uphill by mule, pony, or ox. Often enough, however, the span oxen of Lombardy are not used, but the small farmer will simply harness his cow into the little cart (Plate 38).

It is at Ortisei that the Sasso Lungo first comes into sight, a mass of rock so stupendous that it dominates the whole landscape. To see it from the Suisi Alp above is to see it at its best, for it rises almost immediately from the pastures in a succession of pinnacles and ridges, complex yet coherent, a piece of mountain architecture that is unique (Plate 30). Responsive to every change of atmosphere and lighting, it can vary in a few moments from almost dazzling creamy yellow and grey to cold purple and blue shades under a storm cloud. From this side too it catches the fading sun, and long after the Val Gardena has passed into shade its upper crags can be seen glowing orange in the sunset light.

Its vastness can be set against some of the Alpine giants without fear of being lost. If the Matterhorn rises from its glaciers in a final pyramid of five thousand feet, or the Aiguilles of Chamonix by a similar extent above the Mer de Glace, the three-thousand-foot sweep of bare rock thrown up by the Sasso Lungo from this side is comparable.

Above Santa Cristina is Schloss Fischburg, and near-by the site of the former castle of Oswald von Wolkenstein, the warrior and Minnesänger, whose curious history is set out fully in Gilbert and Churchill. Beyond is the village, formerly Wolkenstein, and now Selva, which is the highest village of the Gardena. The motor road to the Sella leads through it.

But before going up to the Sella Pass to quit the valley, it is as well to visit the smaller gateway to the east, the northern counterpart of the great Pordoi. The Passo Gardena is this gateway between the embattled cliffs of the Sella plateau (Plate 51) and the curious saw-toothed ridges of the Cir, with the black cleft of the famous Adang-Kamin running directly up the centre of the highest peak, a thousand-foot chimney climb, just above the pass. From this peak the eastern mountains—Cristallo, the Pelmo, the Tofane—all stand out on the horizon, whilst to the south-west are new aspects of the Sasso Lungo and Sciliar. It is easy to reach the summit without facing the Adang problem by using a well-designed track finding its way among the southern crags. From the Gardena Pass also is the even rougher track into the Sella under the Pisciadu crags, eventually reaching the Rifugio Boé by stony and desolate corries (Plate 52).

The inn at the pass is an old "hut" of the D. & Oe. A.V., and the Adang-Kamin Book is available. It is one of those Alpine records always interesting to the climber. When I returned to the inn some years ago, after an ascent of the

Adang, I signed the book and was at least in the nine hundred and odds—I forget the exact number. But on looking back the previous English entry was nine years before, in 1937, by John Poole. The intervening years of war had yielded a crop of German and Austrian officers, with one name of special interest, that of Luis Trenker, the Austrian guide, film actor, and author.

Purely as a sight-seeing expedition, a walk from either Santa Cristina or Selva to the northern alps below the Odli group is worth taking. The Sasso Lungo and Sciliar, based upon the broad Suisi Alp, are seen to advantage, and the architecture of the Odli group itself is enhanced, for it is on a smaller scale than that of the Sasso Lungo, and is diminished overmuch from the distant Suisi Alp because of this.

From Ortisei two walks across the Suisi Alp are specially worth doing. The first is to the Sciliar (Schlern), which has given its name to the typical Dolomite rock. It is a flat-topped mountain, and though its southern faces and its north-west angle become steep and craggy, ending in two remarkable pinnacles, it can be climbed from the north-east by paths up the screes and grass. On the plateau a few minutes below the actual summit is a good Alpine inn where a meal or a night's rest can be had.

The summit is one of those places popular with men who enjoy a good rousing panorama. Much of it is distant, and needs a monocular if one is to extract the maximum interest from it. The view extends from the Brenta in the south-west, with the Presanella beyond, to the Ortler, Oetzthal, Stubai, and Zillerthaler Alps in the north. The nearest and most fascinating part of the views is to the east, where Dolomites in serrated ranks stretch from the Odli group to the nearer Sasso Lungo, the Rosengarten and Latemar summits. By walking to the edge of the main plateau, striking views of the valleys open up. From the Sciliar, routes may be made through the passes either to the Sella Pass, beyond the Sasso Lungo group, to the Duron valley and the valley of Fassa, or to Castelrotto.

Another repaying walk from Ortisei or Santa Cristina is wilder, more difficult, and very impressive for its rock scenery. It leads up the great hollow lying between the Sasso Lungo and the Sasso Piatto, into a wilderness of scree flanked by colossal cliffs. After ascending the zigzags for an hour or two beyond the last meadows, the path leads to the Capanna Vicenza (the old Langkofelhütte of the D. & Oe. A.V.) below a peak which rises in the centre of the cirque. On a fine summer's day this amphitheatre can be very hot, the white screes almost as dazzling as a snow slope, and the balcony of the inn consequently a very welcome place to rest awhile, perhaps over a cup of tea "mit rhum", which to my mind is the finest drink in the mountains. The tea is refreshing, whilst the rum is just the thing for any slight queasiness that the altitude and heat together may cause. The view outwards from this gorge is less attractive than the wider panorama of the Sciliar or even of the Suisi Alp, for we are high above the trees and pastures, the foothills to the north are small, and the snows of Austria on the skyline too distant. It is ahead and to the sides that the best scenery lies. Here the complex architecture of the Sasso Lungo can be seen, with its gullies and walls, its great subsidiary pinnacles, its occasional turrets or minarets of gold or grey. The peak rises high into the sky and the impression is of a true mountain mass. From the track, a little higher, the central peak of the corrie no longer hides the Forcella, the gate in the crags between the Sasso Lungo and the Cinque Dita, which is the climax of the walk. But as we slog up the zigzags among the scree and occasional snow beds, above the pass rise the clustered pinnacles of the Cinque Dita, as Gothic as the spires of any village in Gardena. Another half-hour, or perhaps a little more in noonday heat, and we reach the crest of the pass, the old Langkofeljoch, with confident expectation of a wider horizon than we have seen since entering the gorge. We are not disappointed. The steep screes fall away below to the shelving grassland above the Sella Inn, where the long curves of the mountain road come up from Gardena, rise to the pass itself, and then sweep down into the Fassa valley, so far below that it is hidden by the rolling alps around the Col Rodella, a minor summit in the centre of the view (Plate 48). To the left are the Sella Towers, campaniles in true Italianate style, flat-topped and vertical-walled, set against the plateaux of the Sella and the Pordoi (Plate 46). The formation of these masses is quite different from the flying buttresses and steeples of the peaks behind us. A thick layer of softer rock (the Raibl beds of the geologist) lies across these plateau walls, breaking them horizontally in the style of a sandstone district rather than one of limestone. Ahead, and above the Col Rodella, rise distant blue craggy peaks, the northern spurs of the San Martino range, with the Vezzana and Cimon della Pala most clear (Plate 48). But undoubtedly the finest reward of this way to the pass is the head-to-foot picture of the Marmolata, the highest Dolomite, with its long glacier slope gleaming in the sun, and a little rock at its crest giving a hint of the vast precipice of its southern side.

The descent to the Sella Inn from the pass is down screes which can be taken direct in the Lakeland style, or more carefully followed by the track which is worn plain by the passage of many feet, for this walk is one of the best in the region and young Italy on holiday knows it well. Although foreshortened, the Cinque Dita and Sasso Lungo tower above, and a new face is seen, the long eastern aspect of the latter. It is quite different from the obviously complex walls and buttresses we passed in the corrie, and is seen to best advantage from the summit of the Sella Towers. There it shows a broad front, almost unrelieved by pinnacles or buttresses, yet because of this a difficult face for the mountaineer who ventures upon it guideless. Some friends of mine, with only the smallest reserves of food, spent two days trying to descend the Pichl route.

As the Sella Inn is approached, foreshortening helps the Sella Towers, as it hinders the impressiveness of the Sasso Lungo group. For the towers as seen from the pass are liable to be lost against the plateau wall, unless the sun shadows reveal their separate identity. But from the lower level of the inn they stand out apparently higher than the main mass. It is still not evident that they form a sort of pinnacle ridge, but a mile or so down the main road to Gardena this alignment is plainer. That is only one of many instances in the Dolomites where a short walk reveals an utterly different aspect of the same crags or mountains, and therein lies much of their charm (Plate 135). This walk is advisedly taken in the direction described. To reverse it from Sella to Gardena is to have the best views at one's back.

A third walk from the Val Gardena, preferably from Santa Cristina or Selva, is to reach the east end of the Suisi Alp by Monte Pana through the woods, and then contour round the Sasso Lungo by the north and east. This is interesting for its views of the striking north-east buttresses of the peak, where a very good steep climb has been made, in all about a thousand metres high to the ridge. This walk leads eventually through the curious remains of a great rockfall, the Steinernes Stadt, where the outlook to the Odli group, the Cir, and the line of pinnacles on the Sella cliffs all make up yet another landscape worth seeing (Plate 47).

The Sella Pass is not on the great Dolomite Road itself, but is a very significant point in the Western Dolomites. It marks the cleavage between the Ladinian-Germanic peoples of the Gardena and the Italian valley of Fassa.

The Sella Inn, on the highroad a few minutes below the pass, is officially a "hut" of the Italian Alpine Club, though indistinguishable from a normal mountain hotel. It is a very good place indeed for a few days' stay, particularly so for the climber. The Sasso Lungo climbs, the Cinque Dita by the classic Schmitt Kamin and similar east face routes, and the Punta Grohmann are on the one side of the pass, whilst on the other Sella Towers and the Murfreit Tower offer more good rock climbs.

THE VAL DI FASSA

It is easy and wise to journey into Fassa from the Sella Pass by the woods rather than by the main road. Three or four tracks lead down the grassy slopes from the head of the pass, among the larch and pine woods, with views of the curious granitic rocks of the Fassa valley. This sudden change in the immediate surroundings of Fassa from limestone to porphyry and similar rock is very attractive and interesting. It occurs elsewhere, notably near Nova Levante on the Carezza road and above Paneveggio and San Martino. The whole Dolomite region is carried on a great foundation of the reddish porphyry, which contrasts pleasantly with the green woods and alps, and makes for attractive streams whose beds are a mixture of multi-coloured granitic and dolomite pebbles.

The traveller who intends to pick up the motor service en route either for Bolzano to the west or for Cortina and points east will be indifferent as to his choice of village, either Canazei or Campitello being the most convenient from Sella. These villages are also best as a halting place if he intends to explore the Rosengarten by the dramatic northern approach.

The way lies up the five miles of the Duron Thal, easy going in farming country, until a steeper track up the woods at the valley head leads to the Rifugio di Alpe di Suisi, where a halt is convenient. From here a clear track leads to the deeply set Passo di Molignon in an hour, and a descent of screes with another wild pass to be crossed, the Passo di Principe, leads straight into the heart of the remotest part of the Rosengarten, with imposing peaks at all sides. Less than two miles from the pass, by a descending route, the Rifugio di Vajolet is reached, in rock scenery that is as varied and remarkable as any in the whole province. Certainly this inn shares honours with such well-placed huts as the Brentei, in the Val Brenta, the Contrin under the Marmolata, and the Zsigmondy in the Sesto (Sexten) group, as one of those offering most striking aspects of rock architecture to all who care to go, yet without involving anything more than rough walking in the approach. The Vajolet Hut is really three buildings—an inn, a dormitory building, and a small church. A similar grouping is seen at Contrin and elsewhere.

Above, in the east, are the cliffs of the Cima di Pope, from the summit of which, incidentally, the very best general view of the Vajolet Towers is obtained. To the west of the hut rises a steep gorge flanked by the Vajolet Towers on one side, continued in the Croda del Rey Laurino and the Punta Emma of the Catinaccio on the other, ending at the Santner Pass, which is the outlet at this point to the western slopes of the range. A mile past the pass is the Rif. Aleardo Fronza at the end of the path from Carezza al Lago, which hugs the western walls all the way.

At Vajolet the great scoop of bare rock and screes, with these savage crests and steeples on every side, can be an abomination of desolation in dull weather, and little better in the glaring sun of noonday. Atmosphere is everything, for there is no softer foreground of green alp and colourful village to relieve the starkness of the mountains. But when the mists roll down the corries and through the gaps in the mountain wall, and gleams of sun sweep across the intricate architecture of the crags, then the mountains come to life and "music haunts their iron hearts by glimmering ridge and scar".

To see the gradual awakening of the peaks at dawn from such a lonely glen as this is a wonderful visual experience. The bright sky overhead heralds the day, and the first direct rays of the early sun strike the upper crests, which glow dull red against the sky. Gradually the light strengthens, and the red brightens into orange and gold, as the shadows of the peaks against the sun climb down towards the screes. The gold too becomes gradually lost as the sun gathers its full strength, until against a sky of deepening ultramarine the peaks stand dazzling in cream and grey and ivory. The pageant of the dawn is over, the rose glow has gone, but the memory will long remain to anyone who has spent an hour in such a place.

The existence of the Dolomite Road, which carries the traveller quickly into the heart of the Dolomites, can too easily involve missing those finely blended impressions of the mountains that a slower approach can offer. There are other approaches from Bolzano to the north-western groups of the Rosengarten, the Sciliar, and the Sasso Lungo.

For the walker the Val di Tires is one such way into the Rosengarten. The Brenner road is best left about two miles east of Bolzano, at Prato all'Isarco, and either the minor road, or better still the higher paths over the alp, taken to Tires and to the charming village of San Cipriano. Ahead is the line of western cliffs of the Rosengarten, with the great domes of the Catinaccio and the Catinaccio d'Antermoia standing above the general line of minor peaks.

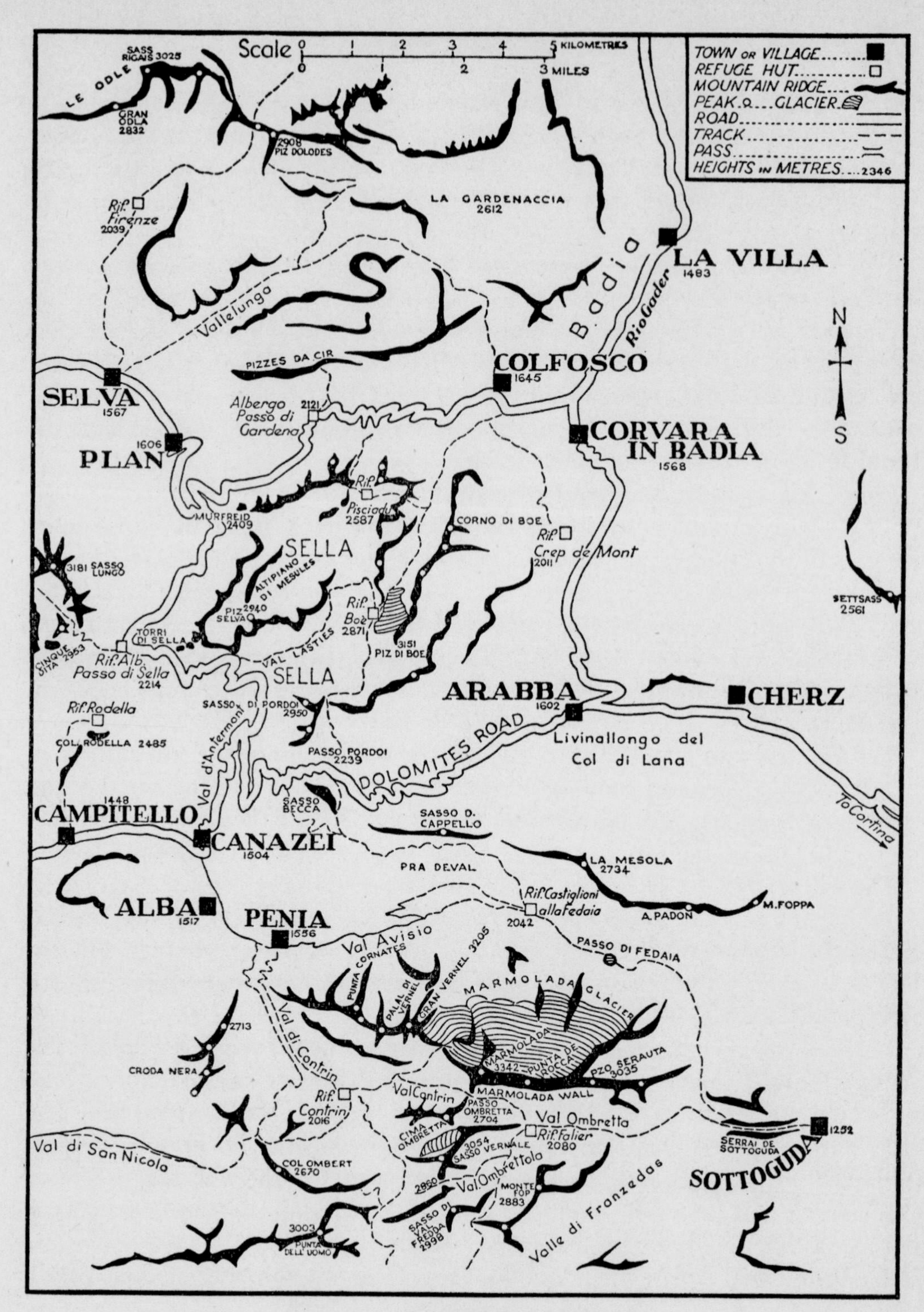

SELLA–MARMOLADA GROUPS

But the thin twisted obelisk of the Delago and the blank, huge Walls of King Laurin grow bigger and more dramatic with every mile, until at the last upper stretches of alp and woodland they tower into the sky. With a stiff pull up to the Laurins Pass, we step into the inner corrie of this group to join the north–south track to Vajolet.

The Vajolet Hut can be approached from the lower villages such as Vigo and Pera, by the Vajolet valley, under the cliffs of Larsec, or better still by the upper path over Ciampedie, a splendid viewpoint for Dirupi di Larsec and indeed for all the southern peaks of the Rosengarten. It was from this pine-covered hill that Mr Arthur Gardner obtained his photograph of Dirupi di Larsec, one of the most beautiful Dolomite views I have ever seen. It is reproduced in his *Art and Sport of Alpine Photography*.

From Vigo or Pera, once the Rosengarten has been explored, the walker can make his way to the Marmolata peaks by the eastern Val di San Nicolo, over the pass of that name, and so into Contrin. But from Campitello the shorter way is along the secondary roadway to Penia, then by the woodland tracks up the Val di Contrin. The former route offers views behind of the Rosengarten, whilst the latter looks out to the Sasso Lungo group; and if the journey is made in late evening, the sunset sky is enriched by these striking crests standing against it.

The Contrin Inn is well placed high up the valley, above the tree-line, with its attendant chapel and small bell-tower built of dolomite. The feature of the view from hereabouts is the vertical Marmolata South Wall seen in profile above the Ombretta Pass.

The hut is liable to be rather full in summer, especially at week-ends, for it is the starting point of the now popularised route to the summit of the Marmolata by the Marmolata Pass, between the Vernel peaks and the main mountain. This is Tuckett's 1872 route but with beaten tracks, iron stanchions on the rocks, and wire handrails at many points. In spite of these elaborate aids to success it is not recommended to the walker unless he is prepared to return by the same way. The northern climbing descent is by a snow and rock ridge leading to the main glacier, which has to be crossed to the Fedaia, and thus is a little more exposed than should be undertaken except by a roped party. Italians do it, sometimes alone and often unroped, but there is danger on the rock ridge and it should be avoided unless a rope is taken. An axe is necessary also in all but the finest conditions.

A journey well worth the effort, and involving no climbing of an exposed

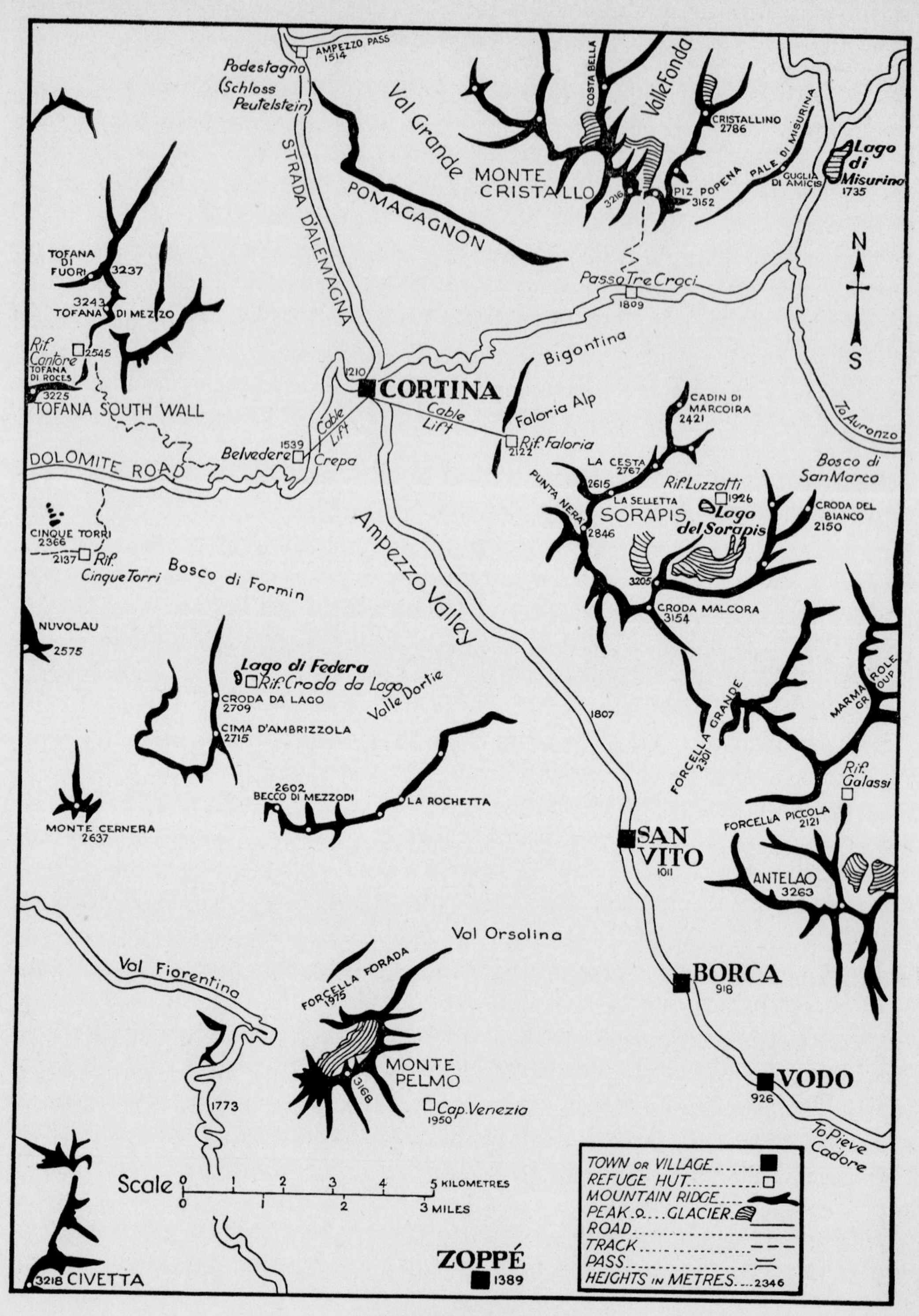

AMPEZZO GROUP

kind, is to leave the Contrin in the early morning for the Ombretta Pass (Plate 62) in time to see sunrise over the Rosengarten, with the complementary silhouettes of the Pelmo and Civetta against the eastern sky from the pass itself (Plate 63). The next part of the route lies down the Ombretta Pass, but if possible a divergence should be made at the pass to ascend, by an easy slope, the Piz Ombretta. The view obtained from this peak of the great South Wall of the Marmolata is full reward for the detour. These cliffs are almost three thousand feet high, as near vertical as makes no matter, and stretch in an unbroken line for over two miles, thus being one of the most considerable masses of rock in the Eastern Alps. The original route up the Wall near the Ombretta is one of the finest climbs in the Dolomites, and is illustrated on Plates 145 to 149.

After spending an hour or two in the ascent of Ombretta and the enjoyment of the Marmolata and Vernel landscape, a return to the pass can be rapidly made, and the walk continued down the Val Ombretta to Pettorina, with continuously changing aspects of the crags, both of the Marmolata di Rocca and of the peaks around the side valley of Ombrettola, until Pettorina is reached. From here it is worth while continuing two miles through the fantastic and narrow gorge of the Serrai di Sottoguda to the village of Sottoguda itself, a convenient halting place.

The disadvantage of a descent to Sottoguda, impressive as the Serrai may be, is that one has arrived at nowhere in particular, and a return to Pettorina must be made before the full circuit of the Marmolata by way of the Fedaia can be completed. Those who prefer the higher passes to valley walking may choose, when halfway down the Ombretta valley, to halt at the Rifugio Falier and turn up the Ombrettola glen, by a track rising steeply to the pass, with an equally steep descent on the western side leading through the subsidiary peaks of the southern Marmolata group, to the Contrin Hut. But this little pass, approached by a steep north-facing ravine, is not one to be attacked in spring when the snows lie heavy, except by fairly experienced parties, properly equipped with axes and either climbing irons or fully nailed boots. The more open Ombretta walk is not so liable to the formation of steep snow slopes.

THE CORTINA DISTRICT

Whatever one may think of Cortina itself, the district accessible from it is one of great distinction. Whilst many of the most striking Dolomite pinnacles are found in ridges or compact groups, such as the long line of San Martino or Brenta peaks, the Sasso Lungo or Sella groups, Cortina is surrounded by massive separate peaks, each rising from fairly low levels and thus giving the impression of really great mountains. The Pelmo and the Civetta are at the extreme range of the Cortina orbit, but they are equalled in grandeur by the ring of peaks to be seen from the Church campanile. Cristallo, Sorapis, Antelao, Tofana each have individuality of design. The first is distinguished by its huge buttresses and its northern glacier; Sorapis by its long subsidiary ridges forming cirques between them, with half a dozen summits of note; Antelao soaring upwards to an irregular cone; whilst the Tofane are bulky domes throwing down tremendous walls to the south.

Among the great peaks are lesser groups of crags, the fine ridge of Pomagagnon alongside Cristallo, and the curious and famous Cinque Torri which seem so huge when we walk closely under them, yet are dwarfed into almost boulder size by the bulk of the Tofane when seen from the Nuvolau. This latter peaklet is noted for its Alpine inn on the summit, incidentally a very good place for morning and evening light effects. The Croda da Lago, with a fairly easy backstairs from the plateau, has a fine east face for the gymnast.

Those who do not care for walking can easily enlarge the views of the valley walls by ascending to two good viewpoints by cable elevator. The first goes to the ridge of Pocol, where stands the War Memorial, and this ridge is best for the outlook to Cristallo and Pomagagnon, Sorapis and Antelao. The second goes to the ridge above the Faloria Alp, and though again good for Cristallo, also looks to the castellated walls of Pelmo, to the Tofane, and to the Punta Nera slopes of Sorapis, which are very near.

The Faloria woods stretching from here to Tre Croci below Cristallo are a charming upland, with ample clearings and little rock saddles to lift the walker over the tree-tops for a sight of the peaks, and no better or pleasanter start to a tour from Cortina is possible. The inns at Tre Croci make a good halting place following a short afternoon walk, but for a full day it is worth walking to the Rifugio Luzzatti (Pfalzgauhütte) in the cirque of ridges that make up the north-west angle of Sorapis, a cirque that has been compared to Gavarnie of the Pyrenees. When continuing from either the hut or Tre Croci after a night's rest, the Misurina Alp is recommended either for its own sake or en route for the Val Sesto (Sexten) peaks.

There are very few lakes in the Dolomites, as in any other limestone region, and such as there are are shallow. The Lake of Alleghe is the largest, deep sunk

3. Fiera di Primiero: Old Houses of Italian Style
4. The same

90. Fiera di Primiero: Old Houses of Austrian Style
91. The same

2. The Peaks of Primiero from Count Welsperg's Park
3. Castello la Pietra

94. A Summer Cottage on the Alp

5. A Forester's Cottage

96. Old Tonadico
97. The same

3. The Cima della Madonna, Sass Maor and Cima Cimerlo from near Tonadico

99. San Martino di Castrozza from the Cima della Madonna

oo. The Wall: the Cimon della Pala
oi. The Wall: the Rosetta and Figlio della Rosetta

102. The Wall: the Pala di San Martino
103. The Wall: the Sass Maor and Cima della Madonna

04. The Peaks of San Martino: Autumn Morning

105. Sunrise on the Cimon della Pala

06. The Ridge of the Cimon
07. From the Bettega Pass

108. Between the Cimon and the Vezzana. The Marmolata is visible left of the deep shadow

ɔ9. The Summit Ridge of the Cimon
ɪo. The Pale di San Lucano

111. From the Cima della Madonna, across the Cismon Glen
112. The Cima di Ball

below the Civetta, and only six other small lakes are found, four of them in the Cortina Alps. Misurina, unfortunately, is spoiled by civilisation. It has a road to one side, hotels at the northern end, and a "grand hotel", the Grand Albergo di Savoia, at the southern end, with a summer-house on an artificial island in the middle. Yet, despite these almost overwhelming handicaps, it still is worth seeing, and on an autumn morning when the mist streamers are drifting among the peaks of Sexten, with the sun glow strengthening behind the Cime di Lavaredo, even the summer-house can be forgotten in the splendour of a new day (Plate 71). But the tiny, reedy Lago d'Antorno a mile farther on still reflects the Cime and has a simpler charm. It lies on the route from Misurina to the Monte Piano, an easy ascent, nowadays even accessible to cars, but with a summit plateau like a miniature Schlern and with the same advantages as a viewpoint. From it the Ampezzo and Sexten peaks stand out well against the sky; Cristallo, the rusty-tinted ridge of the Croda Rossa, the Cime di Lavaredo rather jumbled together, the Cadini spires, and to the south, beyond Misurina, Sorapis, the Croda Malcora of the early travellers. Monte Piano can be descended to Carbonin (Schluderbach), a station on the single-track electric line that runs south to Cortina, for an easy return to civilisation.

This same line is a convenient way to travel to San Vito di Cadore, which is the best starting point either for the walk up to Pelmo on the west or the two passes to the east. The first of these, the Forcella Grande, leads under the great southern cliffs of the Sorapis group to the Valle di San Vito, the Bosco di San Marco, and eventually the Val d'Ansiei, through which runs the motor road from Cortina to Auronzo.

The second, the Forcella Piccola, the little pass, is north of Antelao, and is the starting point for the old route to the summit of the mountain. Once through the pass, the track goes on between the spurs of Antelao and the lone ridges of the Marmarole to the north. A strong walker can reach Pieve di Cadore by this route in the day from San Vito. Pieve is well worth a visit, whether reached in this roundabout way or direct from Cortina by rail or road.

A good deal gentler than any of the foregoing are the more usual and popular walks from Cortina to the west. A flying start is given by the cableway to Crepa, and from this point good tracks lead over to the Cinque Torri, the Nuvolau, and eventually to the Alleghe valley. The section from the Nuvolau to the Colle Santa Lucia north of Alleghe is notable for the fine and unusual views of the Marmolata and the Pelmo.

The Ampezzo Pass, between Cristallo and the Croda Rossa, marks a division

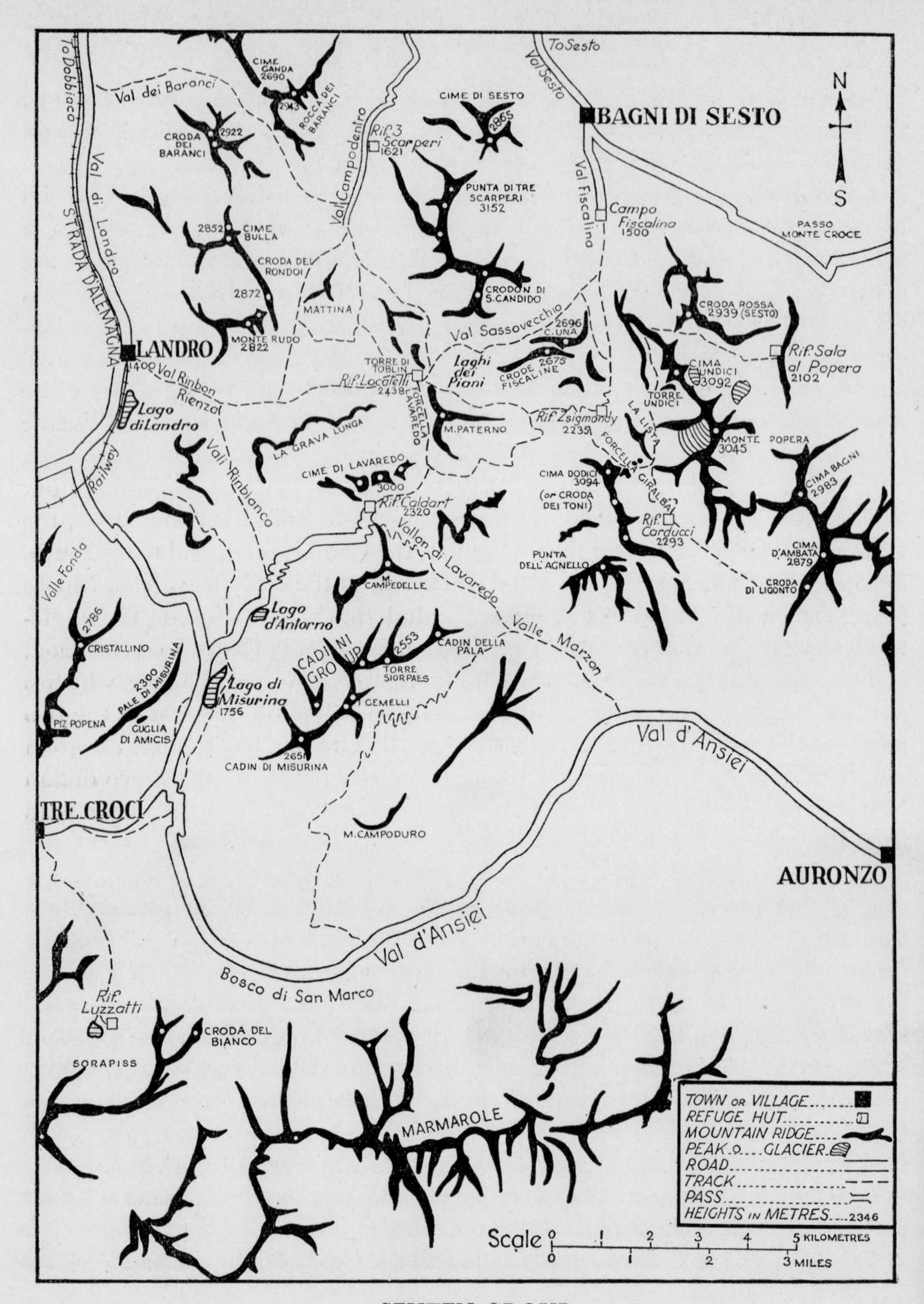

SEXTEN GROUP

between Italian and Germanic areas almost as decisively as the Sella Pass does in the west. The Landro valley (Höhlensteinthal) is one of great beauty and its principal feature is the Lago di Landro (Dürrensee) (Plate 87).

Landro is the starting point of a good approach to the Dolomites of the Val Sesto (Sexten), where some of the most ferocious peaks are to be seen. At the head of the Val Rinbon which penetrates the eastern crags of the valley tower the Tre Cime di Lavaredo, and the approach to them is by the pine woods alongside the wide watercourse, until the glen divides, two miles from Landro. Here the Valle di Rinbianco can be taken if a southern approach to the Cime is preferred, for at its head the track joins the narrow road that has in recent years been carried as far as the Rifugio Caldart (formerly Principe Umberto), almost directly under the southern cliffs of the Cima Grande (Grosse Zinne). This hut is not only a comfortable place in itself but an excellent viewpoint for the steeples of the Cadini group to the south (Plate 74). An easy stroll from the hut to Monte Campedelle further enhances this group. All round the Cime runs the Pian or tableland on which the peaks rise (Plate 75), and the wanderer can find many good places from which to see and study the ridges of the Cima Dodici (Zwölferkofel) and the Monte Paterno (Paternkofel).

The deep valley running south to Auronzo, shown on Plate 73, is another of the landscapes seen from this plateau, and the misty-bright conditions of that day showed a subtle range of tones in the receding blue-purple silhouettes of the pine slopes and craggy hills.

Between the Paterno and the Cima Piccola (Kleine Zinne) is the Lavaredo Pass, and an almost level track north reaches the Rifugio Locatelli (Drei Zinnenhütte) in half an hour from the pass.

If instead of turning up the Valle di Rinbianco the direct route up the Val Rinbon is taken, the track leads straight to the Locatelli Hut.

The view of the Tre Cime from this point is very fine (Plate 79), for the great north walls are visible from head to foot and the "impossibility" of the face of the Cima Grande can be fully understood. It was climbed shortly before the recent war by three guides using enormous quantities of rope, pitons, and karabiners, and has been repeated on several occasions.

SEXTEN DOLOMITES

The Sexten group of peaks are the most northerly of all the Italian Dolomites, and are usually considered to begin at the Cime di Lavaredo, with the adjacent Monte Paterno (Paternkofel). But the best of all this group are the great summits towering over the Sexten and Fischlein glens (Val Sesto and Val Fiscalina), the Elfer, Zwölfer, and Einser, with the highest of all, the Dreischusterspitze. In such an exclusively Austro-Tyrolese district as this there is little excuse for the adoption of Italianised names, except for the Cime and other peaks of the old frontier.

Once we are at the Lavaredo Pass, the Cortina orbit is quitted, the motor roads to viewpoints and huts are thankfully left behind, and a wilder, more primitive country is in front. The *Schneehuhn* and even the *Gems* have not entirely deserted these north-western mountains.

This is an old and a famous battlefield of the Great War. Here among the cliffs of the Paternkofel and at the head of the pass between the latter and the Oberbachernspitzen, below the Zwölfer wall, are traces of old gun emplacements, tunnels, and redoubts built in the rock, outworks, observation posts, machine-gun nests, all looking like a deserted city. The old Zsigmondy Hut below the pass was demolished by shellfire in 1915, and the Drei Zinnen Hut on the Toblinger Riedel was also destroyed. When the former was rebuilt in 1927, the honoured name of Zsigmondy was erased and that of Mussolini substituted. Since the recent war it has again been named, this time as the Rifugio Zsigmondy-Comici, and in the common room, among the chamois heads, the ropes and pitons, and the sporting rifles, are portraits of both, a striking and salutary contrast. On the one side is the photograph of the modern, the Trieste guide, with glaring eyes and an heroic pose; on the other, a picture revealing the gentle, sensitive face of the young Viennese physician of half a century ago.

Each was a product of his age. Comici was a very brave and accomplished cragsman, let there be no doubt of that, but a creation of Fascismo. The sympathy of English climbers will lie more with the memory of Zsigmondy and his like, who climbed the mountains for love of them, not for notoriety or gold, and who, being Austrian, seemed to stand between Prussia on the one hand and Italy on the other, avoiding the arrogance of the one, yet keeping their courage and competence; avoiding the instability of the other, yet keeping all of their charm and courtesy.

It is a rewarding journey to the Zsigmondy Hut, either from Landro by the Val Rinbon and the Alpe di Pian or from Misurina by the Pian de Cengia and the Forcella della Croda dei Toni or the Passo del Rio di Sopra. Either pass is easy, with superb views to the Auronzo peaks in the south and the Elferkofel

(Plate 76) and Monte Popera ridges (Plate 77) to the north-east. The hut is built on a flat shoulder of the Einser massif, and from its windows one can look down the Fischleinthal (Val Fiscalina), across foothills to the distant snows of the Venediger.

Across a wide sweep of scree is the fine curve of the Forcella Giralba, the escape pass from Sesto to Giralba and Auronzo, flanked by the stupendous crags of the Zwölferkofel, looking utterly inaccessible, and the flatter plateau of Monte Popera. The saw-tooth profile of Elfer is to the east, and the hut for grandeur of situation rivals, if it does not exceed, the Rifugio Vajolet or the Capanna Vicenza under the Sasso Lungo.

It has one disadvantage to those who seek to return to the Cortina road, it is a thousand feet below the Passo del Rio, which leads shortly to the Forcella del Pian de Cengia. But the return is well worth this initial slog, especially if, as I did, the traveller engages a porter from the hut to carry his heavy sack to the pass. This porterage cost a mere 300 lire (about 3*s.*) and was worth every bit of it!

The Forcella opens out a fine view of the pinnacle ridges and supporting peaks of the Dreischusterspitze (Plate 83), and the narrow track from it skirting the Paterno cliffs looks over the small tarns of the Alpe dei Piani, and through the gorge of the Altensteinthal (Val Sassovecchio) the snows of Austria gleam again on the skyline.

The Rifugio Antonio Locatelli (Drei Zinnen Hut), a large, well-equipped, and popular place, was, like the Zsigmondy, rebuilt on the site of the old hut. From it a level mile of plateau stretches to the foot of the Cime, La Grava Lunga—the Long Screes—but westwards the edge of the plateau dips with remarkable suddenness into the head of the Val Rinbon. The most repaying route lies down the zigzags of this steep slope, its rocks underfoot covered with bilberries and mosses, among larch and pine clumps to the valley floor, with its wide flood-created stream bed, of screes, boulders, and silt. Above the ranks of trees rises the flat top of Monte Piano, and from the foot of the valley we can see the distant Croda Rossa, with its distinctive red ochre summit rocks, the "mount of sacrifice" of the old pioneers (Plate 85).

The track winds pleasantly through the woods, which are never sufficiently thick to obscure either the Croda ahead, the curious campaniles of the flanking cliffs, or the spiked columns of the Cime di Lavaredo that still rise, in distorted perspective, above the lip of the plateau (Plate 86).

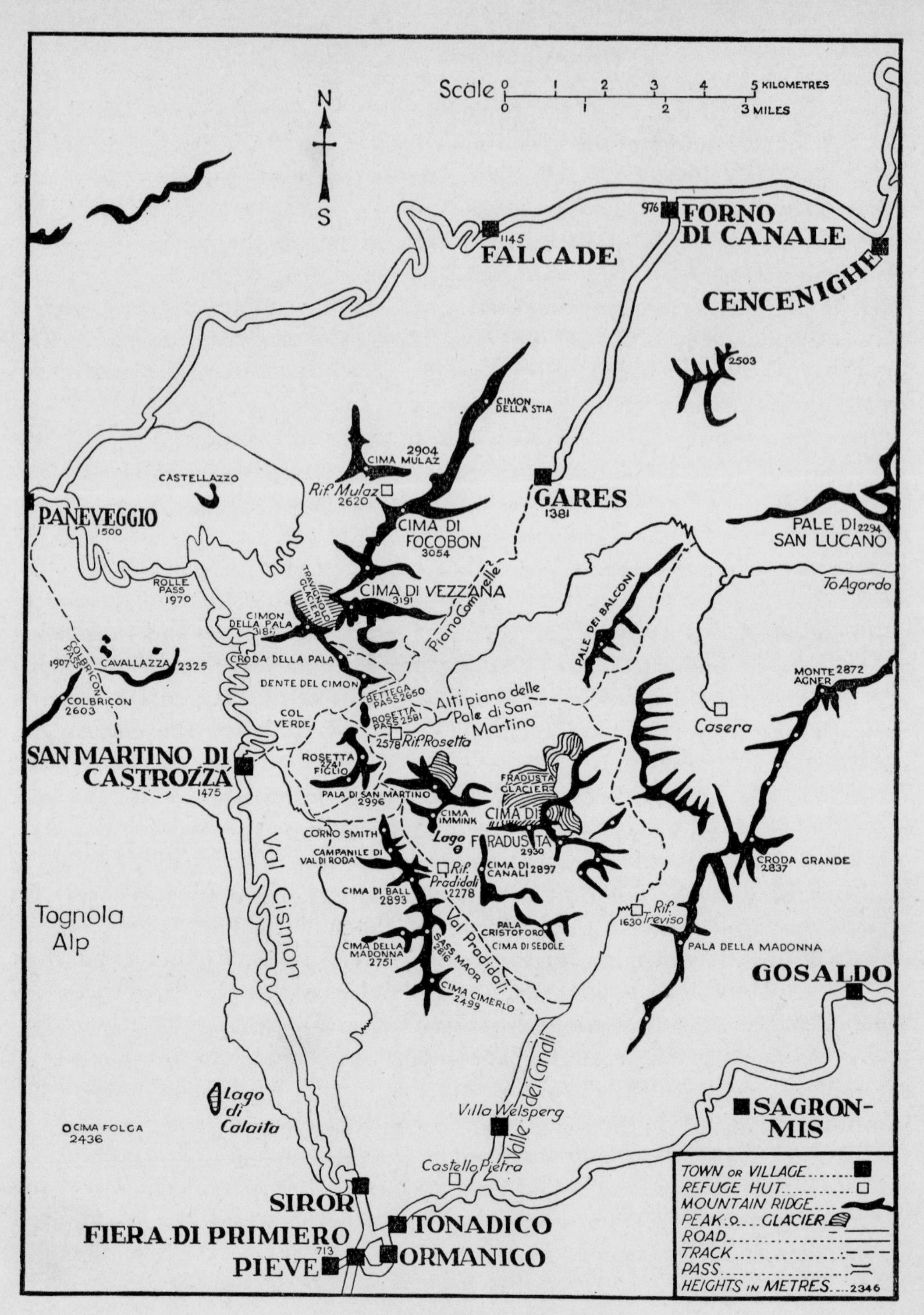

SAN MARTINO GROUP

PRIMIERO AND SAN MARTINO

The Dolomite connoisseur will have difficulty in deciding which of the seven main masses has the greatest charm for him. Gardena has its Sasso Lungo, the Rosengarten its Vajolet Towers, the central group its Marmolata; Cortina points with pride to Cristallo or Pelmo, Sexten to the Dreischusterspitze or the Zwölfer.

But it is possible that his choice will eventually lie between the Brenta and the Primiero peaks. Each has its claims. Incidentally, whatever disputes may have overlaid the northern hills, here at least the peaks are "*ganz italienisch*", as a German professor was careful to admit in his book on the district. All peaks are and always were named in Italian, although only a few of those at Primiero were on the old Italian frontier, whilst the Brenta were wholly inside Austria.

The Brenta to the west and the Primiero peaks to the east are the most southerly of Dolomites. Their lower slopes that look to the sun grow maize and corn, chestnuts and vines, to contrast with the north-facing slopes of pines.

Primiero can be approached by motor from the Val di Fassa to Paneveggio, over the Rolle Pass, and down through San Martino. This approach has one tremendous claim—the breath-taking view of the Cimon at the head of the pass, where there is no mistaking the rightness of its title "*il Cervino delle Dolomiti*". But with the exception of this one splendid view, the approach that is the most dramatic is by the Val Sugana. From Trento by coach, Primiero can be reached in about four hours and San Martino an hour later. I went up by this route in late autumn a few years ago, and recall few approaches to the mountains that were finer.

A great blanket of heat lay over the Trento as I waited for the post bus that ran, they told me, every evening into the mountain village I was seeking. At last it came into the sandy side of the Piazza near the sparkling ornate fountain, and I left the shelter of my pavement table, paid for the brave Italian effort to provide me with English tea, and slung my old rucksack into the back of the bus. It filled up with a group of country people—a few peasant women with bulging net shopping bags, a fat nun telling her beads and rolling her eyes, a village priest in shovel hat, an old man with his grandchild going back to his village, a Franciscan friar in brown dusty habit and sandals, and lastly the cheerful guard, with an honest, open countenance and his newspaper *Il Carabinieri di Lenin* (!!) tucked under his arm to read on the journey.

It was cooler as we were driven, with the *élan* that every driver seems to have, up the dusty road into the hills of the Val Sugana. Rich autumn was on every hand. Vineyards hung with black grapes; maize ripened to gold in the fields; here and there tobacco leaves dried on the farm balconies, above the loggia decorated, as it invariably was, by a carefully trained vine forming a shady porch. Up hill and down dale we went for two hours or so through little villages of stucco and pantiles that might well have been there since Roman days. Then, with a sudden turn up the windings of the road engineered in a great limestone cliff, we found ourselves amongst the vast fortifications of Primolano, now half demolished, but speaking of impregnability in the days when artillery and not aircraft dominated the valley defiles on the Austro-Italian frontier of 1914.

The sun sank into the mists, the heat faded with the light, as we climbed steadily up a stupendous gorge with the pine crests of limestone crags a thousand feet above our heads and the mountain stream a thousand feet below.

The gorge ended and ahead we at last saw the lights of Primiero, on a plain guarded on every side by high peaks clear in the moonlight, with this gorge and a high mountain pass beyond as the only approaches.

Lenin's rifleman (or was he only a fellow-traveller?) was courtesy itself. He recommended, and rightly, an excellent little inn by the riverside, had a word with the innkeeper to ensure that the Englishman would be well cared for, and went his separate way.

It seemed next day that my village was little changed from the Middle Ages, when priest and peasant, soldier and robber baron were all to be found in this secret valley.

Much of the ancient history of Primiero can be read in its face, its houses, churches, and inns. It was at one time a frontier town of the Venetian republic, later an outpost of the Austrian Empire. In the Middle Ages its silver mines brought prosperity and fine houses were built. Because the mine-workers were German, a stone-built Gothic church arose with a tall spire that looks strange in the landscape of Italy, though it would pass unremarked in the northern glens.

Primiero and its attendant villages, Tonadico, Transaqua, Ormanico, Pieve, and Siror, are overlooked by the ancient castle, the stronghold of the lords of the valley, the Welspergs. Castel Pietra is falling into shapeless ruins, but it still stands like an eagle's nest on a great crag at the entrance to the Val di Canali, guarding the enchanting view that made Leslie Stephen stop to feel his heart beat the quicker at such beauty:

> "The stream which watered it, sparkling with the incomparable brilliancy characteristic of the Dolomite regions, flows through a level plain of the greenest turf, dotted occasionally with clumps and groves of pines that have strayed downwards from the bounding slopes. Such a meadow as that I was crossing would have been a commonplace pasturage in Leicestershire. Contrasting it with the mighty cliffs that enclosed it on every side, it was a piece of embodied poetry; such a park as we may hope to meet in the Elysian fields; a park as much like its British representative as an angel to a country gentleman. The difference lay principally in the system of fences adopted in the two cases. Here it was formed by one of those gigantic walls that almost oppress the imagination by their stupendous massiveness. I was evidently contemplating one of the great scenic effects of the Alps, not to my taste rivalling Grindelwald, Macugnaga or Courmayeur, yet in its own style almost unique."

Of a certain pass in Switzerland Arnold wrote a lament at the changes in a mere twenty years of tourists' visits and hotel-keepers' enterprise. Primiero has had a happier fate. Stephen's view is still there. I think the most impressive of all the astonishing things about this region was just this one fact. It is everything that Stephen said about it. It is a mystery, an enchanted valley; time has stood still.

In the pines is the woodman's hut, or is it perhaps the gingerbread house? Up on the sunny alp, among an orchard of apple trees, is a tiny two-roomed summer chalet, with half a dozen white rabbits playing around a small yellow-haired child. From every clearing in the forest can be seen the ruined castle gleaming on its rock, and behind it the tall ghostly peaks, the barrier between this unspoilt fragment of fairyland and the hotels and shops of San Martino di Castrozza.

* * * *

San Martino was the patron saint of publicans, and at the village of that name above Primiero he certainly has done well for his children. The Palazzo Sass Maor, the Grand Albergo delle Alpi, the Belvedere, and a dozen others proclaim this village as another resort of fashionable Italy, another Madonna di Campiglio or Cortina. Yet it is not to be utterly despised, for it is cool, it is easy to get out of, and it is west of the San Martino Wall.

This last quality is no mean one. It offers a royal magnificence of sunset lighting. The shapes of the peaks, standing as they do in line, from the Cimon della Pala to the Cima della Madonna, are in themselves a splendid sight at any time of day. But when the sun is low, they take on those incomparable rose tints to rival the Rosengarten itself as the towers glow against the sky. The colours inspire the artist and defeat the photographer. Memory alone for most men remains true, and the only writer who has done justice in words to such a scene is an Italian, the great Guido Rey. May I quote from Mr Eaton's sympathetic translation?

> "The mountains are aglow with their own light . . . at the supreme moment the wondrous forms of the ancient towers, palaces, and temples reappear as if by magic; the dead castles come to life again, the battlements are crowned with shining breastplates and sparkle with lances and swords; the blind loopholes are endowed with sight and the deep caves reveal their treasures. Amid the smoke of the conflagration and the blood-red glare of the final hour one seems to hear the shock of arms, the shouts of combatants, the call of trumpets, the peal of bells and hymns of praise proclaiming the ancient virtues and the eternal beauty of this earth. It is a heroic hour; I fancied I was witnessing the tragic end of an old line overwhelmed by Fate."

Those words were perhaps prophetic, as applied to this valley, for within a year after they were published Italy was at war and San Martino utterly destroyed. Gone with the dust of the Austrian Empire went the old impressions of the village on a summer's evening, of which Rey too wrote: "There were seen white dresses, and fresh smiling faces, the flash of pince-nez and the sparkle of uniforms . . . whilst the soft notes of a Viennese waltz floated through the tall lighted windows of the terrace on to the perfumed air."

Mussolini's Italy rebuilt San Martino, and luck alone saved it from a second destruction. Yet behind the peaks that glow in the sunset a modern field of warfare was found, and in Bill Tilman's book of his work in the Dolomites with the *partisani* he tells of the fires lit on the Altipiano, to guide the planes flying in with vital supplies, whilst he and his Italians waited in the snows.

Peace has come again to the peaks of Primiero, and the pleasant paths and the elegant climbs are still there to be followed by those who care for them.

San Martino, like Paneveggio on the other side of the pass, was originally an isolated hospice, built and maintained under authority of the Prince Bishop, to give shelter to travellers and their beasts in the days when it was something of an undertaking to go from Primiero to Fassa. Even in the middle of last century the light to guide travellers who came over the crest of the pass was nightly placed in a window. By the 'nineties two other hotels had been built, run by Herr Panzer, described by one visitor as a "fat and loathsome individual, the chief propagandist for D. & Oe. A.V. German *kultur* in the district". The advent of the motor car, the opening up of the Dolomite Road in later years, gave the stimulus to the development of San Martino as a holiday resort.

How often it happens that an event of this kind is the salvation of some old place, because the tide of life passes straight past it. Primiero has been saved by this opening up of San Martino, and so retains much of its old atmosphere, except in the high street of the town, where *il turismo* prevails. But up in the village streets of nearby Pieve, where the tall steeple stands above old houses and the terraced fields rise to the woods, there is nothing handed over either to modernisation, nor has it the curiously ossified state of a place bristling with "show places" suitably labelled. Primiero is natural, a little squalid in parts but at least containing a genuine Italian rural community. Under the shade of a balcony, perhaps, an old woman uses a traditional tool for hand-carding coarse wool or goat hair; another halts for a rest with her heavy pannier of apples; a small girl drives a few goats to milking; a sled drawn by a mule or ox passes by, laden with hay.

The more isolated villages of Transaqua, Siror, Ormanico, or Tonadico are the same. Narrow winding streets, cobbled paths, lead among barns and cattle sheds which alternate with peasants' cottages and galleried tenements. A little village square has its cattle trough, and a general-purpose fountain running into it, where the women draw water or wash clothes. And at intervals through the gaps in the tall houses can be seen a steep ridge of pine woods, or a fragment of the blue sky broken by the pale towers of the Sass Maor, the Madonna, or Cima Cimerlo.

The Cismon valley is remarkable for its contrasts. They do not lie solely in those between the modern six-storey San Martino hotels and ancient Primiero, but also in the landscape. For here is the sharp change from a Lombardy vegetation and climate, around Primiero, to the Tyrolese wood and pasture on the hills. The corn and maize grow in the fields of the valley, the chestnuts and fruit trees spread up the south-facing hillsides, yet on the opposing slopes, only a few hundred feet above the maize, are the tall larches and among them patches of green, fresh grazing land.

Moreover, as another and even greater contrast, the wall of dolomite, from the Cimon to the Cimerlo, is the last formidable outwork of the whole dolomite region. Beyond the moat of the Cismon no more dolomite or even limestone is seen to the south and west. Red porphyry ridges stretch from the head of the Rolle Pass for many miles westward, and south of them, opposite the Wall, are rolling foothills rising only rarely above two thousand metres in an occasional craggy top of this rock. The crags of Cavalazza and Colbricon would be striking enough in any district were it not for the drama of the Wall. But this opening to the west is partly the cause of the fine sunset glory of the Wall. In more enclosed dolomite glens the low sun casts the shadows of one ridge across all but the higher crests of that opposite, whilst here the dying sun lights up the head-to-foot height of the crags.

All too often the main road to the Rolle Pass is white with dust and noisy with cars. To see the Wall, a quieter way on the western hills is advised. Good paths lead up to the Tognola Alp, which is nearest to the southern end of the ridge, with little more than two hours' easy walking to that pleasant region in any mountain district where the trees thin out into clumps and the great peaks rise above them in a contrast of colour, tone, and line.

Another way, which is incidentally the finest walking route to Paneveggio, is north-west to the Colbricon Pass and its small tarns. From here for the best views of the Cimon the ridge can be traversed to the Rolle Pass itself, or the tracks of the lower slopes taken to the same place if the heat makes the climber reluctant to struggle up the thousand-foot slope to the ridge.

The peaks from these viewpoints look formidable indeed, and it is no surprise that the key to their conquest was not at first easily found. In the old days the natural approach to them was from Paneveggio, and the early travellers attempted (and eventually succeeded) in forcing steep, Alpine-type approaches up the north-facing glacier of Travignolo, but with some dangers of stonefall from the impending crags.

The discovery of the weaknesses in the western wall, the steep but easy way through the Rosetta Pass, and later the Bettega Pass between the Rosetta and the ridges of the Cimon opened up the "easy backstairs" to most of the peaks at the northern end. Similarly, the route into the high corrie of Pradidali, with its tiny tarn, was the comparable approach from the Val di Canali, and the Comelle Pass by the Altipiano the approach from or escape to Gares.

The walker from San Martino can easily ascend the Rosetta by the first route, which goes up steeply through the pine woods across the Cismon, first to

Col Verde, a shoulder of the mountain where for many years stood a small (and welcome) restaurant. This was burned down in the recent war and has not yet been rebuilt. The Rosetta path turns up screes, among the irregular crags of this slope to the pass. From here only a short and very easy slope, of scree or snow, according to the season, goes to the summit of the mountain that from San Martino looked quite inaccessible to other than skilled cragsmen. An interesting ascent for the latter is on this face thrown down to San Martino by the Figlio, the subsidiary peak.

It is a worthwhile journey to the Rosetta for the superb views which it gives of its neighbours—the Pala itself with its attendant pinnacles, the ridge of the Cima di Ball, and the imposing cliffs of the Cimon. Just below the pass on the east is the comfortable Rosetta Hut.

The approach by the southern route to Pradidali is also worth making, though it is not done conveniently from San Martino, whence a very long circuit is necessary to reach the Val di Canali itself. But experienced and strong walkers may like to take the rough, exciting short cut along the southern flank of the Rosetta and through the Passo di Ball. But such a route as this is one for good weather and experienced men. The Pradidali Hut is an excellent base for climbers who intend to make expeditions at this end of the group. A useful high-level track runs between the two huts.

The Bettega Pass is to the north of the Rosetta Pass and is a little more awkward to reach. Soon after passing the Col Verde, an inconspicuous track diverges from the Rosetta route, up easy rock slabs with superb views of the Cimon crags (Plate 105). At the summit of the pass the ground falls away to the Altipiano and the Comelle Pass, whilst the horizon line is of the distant Cortina peaks (Plate 107). This pass is the key to the ascent of the Cimon by the easiest route.

THE BRENTA GROUP

The Brenta are aloof from the main Dolomite area, for they are some miles west of the Adige, hidden away behind the ridges of Monte Gazza and La Paganella. They stand as a long saw-tooth ridge, about seven or eight miles long in its main central part, though with decreasing heights along the ridge for double that distance.

They are distinctive among the Dolomites for their larger glaciers and longer ice couloirs, which makes them intermediate between the pure rock peaks of the east and the more normal "Alpine" peaks of the Lombard group standing

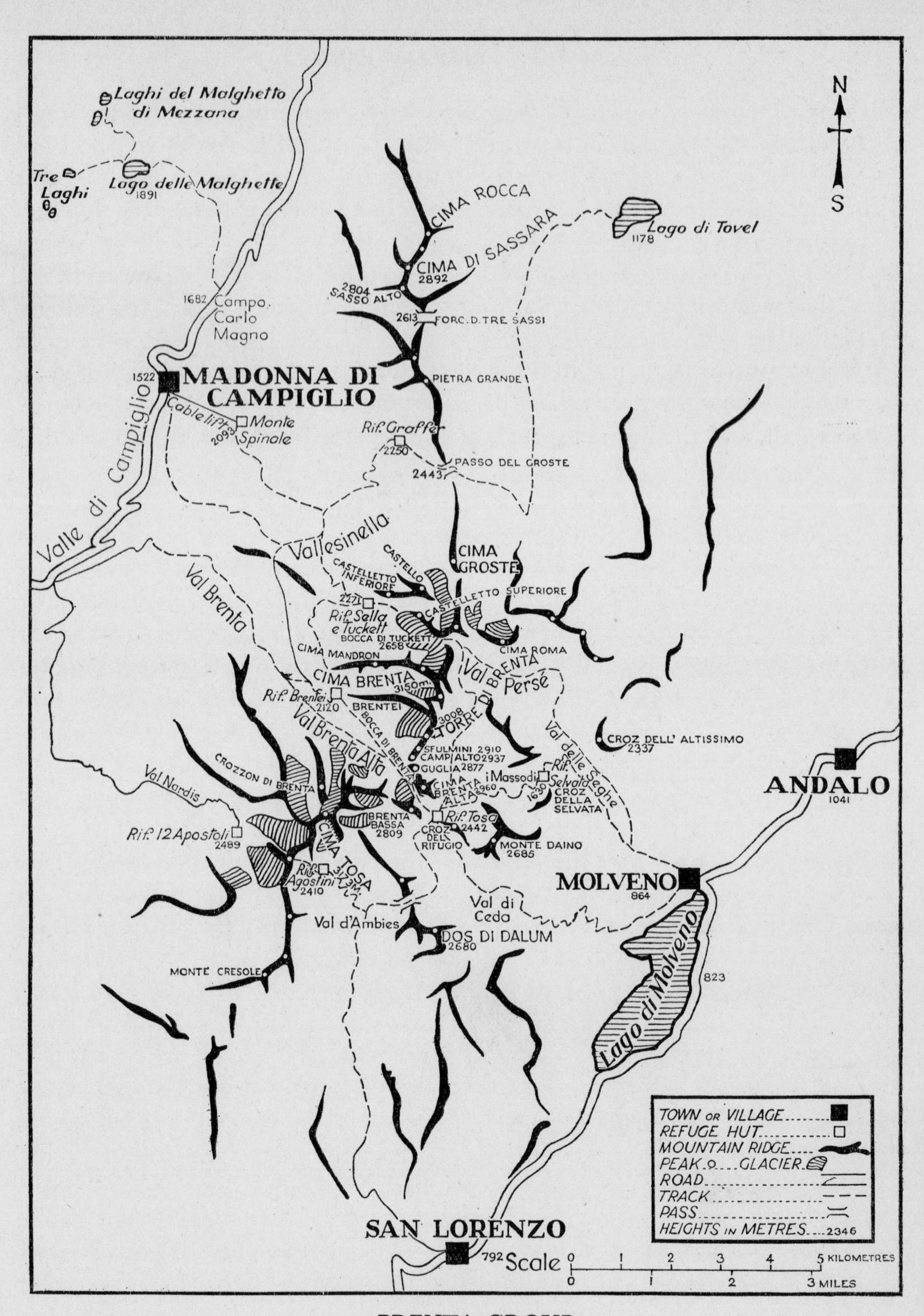

BRENTA GROUP

across the Val di Genova on the west, the granite peaks of Adamello, the Care Alto, and Presanella (Plate 114).

The great ice couloir of the Cima Tosa, which runs from the snow-capped summit to the Vedretta del Crozzon no less than nine hundred metres lower, is unequalled in the Dolomites (Plate 113). This highest peak of the group is a worthy rival to the Marmolata itself, for though it has no southern cliffs to compare in breadth, its colossal northern buttress of the Crozzon, with a three-thousand-foot wall sweeping into the Val Brenta, gives a climb longer than the South Wall routes, and an aspect from below that equals even the Cimon della Pala from the Rolle Pass (Plate 116).

The Cima Brenta, a very easy mountain by any standards, is well worth a visit for its superb and wide-ranging views. It is, perhaps, superior in this to the Cima Tosa, for whilst to the south from the Cima only the hazy plains of Italy can be seen, the Brenta has that quadrant of its view well filled by the Tosa and its buttresses (Plate 113), whilst the extreme limits of the northern horizon are the snow peaks of Austria.

The Brenta group is really best considered as two massifs, the peaks of the Cima Brenta and those of the Tosa, divided by the Val Brenta and that sword-cut of a pass, the Bocca di Brenta. Each has its complex and important buttresses, its attendant pinnacles. With these the Cima Brenta is best supplied, and especially dramatic are the vigorously carved turrets between it and the Bocca. In line these are the Torre di Brenta, the Sfulmini, the Campanile Alto, the Campanile Basso (formerly the Guglia), and the Brenta Alta (Plate 120). The Guglia was the last of the great Dolomite pinnacles to be ascended (see page 79), and even the normal route is still one of the most exacting ascents in the whole of the region.

This line-abreast of striking pinnacles looks equally well from either the upper Val Brenta, preferably on the Crozzon side, or from the Busa degli Sfulmini. The name of the Guglia is seen to be most appropriate from the latter side.

North of the Cima Brenta lie another smaller group of pinnacles, though less striking in form, across the second important pass of the ridge, the Bocca di Tuckett (Plate 125). This pass, named in honour of the old pioneer F. F. Tuckett, is rather more difficult than the Bocca di Brenta, though there is not much to choose. Each is a snow pass on the north-western sides even in the hottest summer. In fact, in the hot summer the slopes are at times bare ice, and the angle here and there can be steep enough to make the vibram-shod traveller wish for nails at least. The slopes are safe enough, if awkward for a few steps, and both are really the merest attenuated shadows of glacier passes compared with those of the high Alps. But the flanking cliffs are so high and the passes so narrow that they should on no account be omitted from a tour.

It is also pleasant to approach the Brenta from the east, by Molveno, a well-situated Italian resort on the banks of the lake of that name, though its altitude (864 metres) is low for comfort in summer. The best line of approach is by the well-trodden track through the Val di Ceda, the Pozza Tramontana, and the gap between the Brenta Bassa and the Croz del Rifugio. Tosa rises finely above the Pozza Tramontana, a high plateau, and the situation, in the gap, of the Rifugio Pedrotti alla Tosa is very unusual (Plate 123). On a rock shelf a few hundred feet below is the old Tosahütte of the D. & Oe. A.V., now closed. From this point the full impressiveness of the narrow Bocca between its two-thousand-foot walls is seen (Plate 126). The pass is less than fifty feet wide and only a half-mile away, reached by a track that winds along one of the terraces formed naturally by the dolomite stratification.

The Pedrotti Hut is a good base for the climbs around the Bocca, both on the Campanili and on Tosa. Moreover, it marks the start of the very good high-level route northwards to the Tuckett Pass.

From the Bocca the descent is at first down snow or ice, with a short and easy rock step, to the worn path along the screes at the foot of the Campanili, and soon afterwards to the upland shelf of the Brentei, on which is the new Brentei Hut, well placed for a head-to-foot view of the profile of the Crozzon (Plate 116) and naturally the base for climbers who make the ascent of the Crozzon by that buttress or by the ice couloir. From this point another high-level route, the counterpart of that leading to the Tuckett Pass on the east, traverses easily round the flanks of the Cima Brenta, to the Tuckett Hut, below the pass of that name. Actually here, as at the Bocca di Brenta, there are two huts, the Quintino Sella Hut of the old Trentine Alpine Society, and the Tuckett Hut which was erected by the German and Austrian Alpine Club. They are only a few yards apart, and the latter is nowadays really an annexe to the Sella Hut, but the Italians have courteously preserved the memory of the Englishman who was so distinguished a member of the German and Austrian Alpine Club (Plate 124).

The walker who is able to spend two or three days at these levels should certainly make the round tour by these high-level tracks, and only then descend from either the Brentei or the Sella-Tuckett, into the wooded Vallesinella, and

3. The Cima Tosa from the Cima Brenta

114. Across the Val Campiglio from the Cima Brenta: the Adamello-Presanella Group

5. Sunrise: Cima Margarita

116. Sunrise: Crozzon di Brenta

117. Crags of the Cima Brenta Alta

118. The Torre di Brenta from the Campanile Basso (Guglia di Brenta)

19. The Campanile Alto from the Guglia di Brenta

120. The Torri, Sfulmini and Campanili di Brenta, Guglia on the right

121. Afternoon Mists, the Crozzon di Brenta

122. In the Val Brenta

23. The Pedrotti and Tosa Huts with the Croz del Rifugio

124. The Sella and Tuckett Huts

25. The Bocca di Tuckett, with the Castelletto Superiore, Cima Sella and Lower Rocks of the Cima Brenta, from the Balcony of the Sella Hut

126. The Bocca di Brenta

7. Afternoon Mists: the Val Brenta and Crozzon

128. Sunset behind Presanella

so to Madonna di Campiglio. This Alpine resort, also originally built around an ancient hospice, is very similar in type to San Martino, or indeed any popular Alpine hotel village. It is unnecessary again to give the advantages and disadvantages of such useful places. Sufficient to say that it has all mod. con., including a cable elevator to the edge of Monte Spinale, the officially approved viewpoint. The wise man will not disdain the cable lift here, any more than at Ortesei, the Fedaia, or Cortina. For to ascend easily, pass a pleasant hour or two at the summit restaurant or in "skilled lounging" over the plateau, and then descend leisurely through the woods is a very good way of spending an off day. After all, there are dozens of other good viewpoints where no such mechanical aids exist. Among them, near Campiglio, are the small lakes on the hills to the west, a few of which offer a beautiful foreground to the grim line of dolomite across the valley, and are equally attractive to the photographer, the artist, or the simple devotee of fine scenery.

The Exploration of the Dolomite Peaks

EARLY MOUNTAINEERING

WHILST Switzerland was well known to travellers in the eighteenth century, and the first half of the nineteenth century saw a good deal of exploration of the heights, either by passes or by actual ascents of summits, the Dolomites remained hidden away from the line of traffic through the Adige, and both the Rosengarten and the Brenta were late in being developed.

The other and equally frequented approach, from Venice to Austria, led naturally through Cortina d'Ampezzo, where the ring of fine peaks could not be missed and helped to make it the classic centre. So much so, that fifty years after the first explorations, the Rev. W. A. B. Coolidge, corresponding with an expert friend when collecting material for his monumental *Alps in Nature and History*, was told that there were no dolomites save in the region of Cortina. Coolidge writing in 1907 (!) comments with obvious irony that "the present writer felt quite certain, in consequence of his hasty journey through the district in 1876, that there were dolomites elsewhere than at Cortina, and investigation showed this to be the case".

As we shall see, by 1907 all peaks, campaniles, minor nodules, and excrescences had been ascended, and the whole region from the Brenta to Sexten was equipped with guides, huts, paths, etc., to serve the multitude of Austrians and Germans who spent holidays in the mountains, and the discriminating few Englishmen who penetrated the icy curtain that stopped so many from passing the Swiss border.

It was very different in 1857, the year when the first dolomite mountain was ascended. The honour fell to John Ball, the first President of the Alpine Club: botanist, geologist, and mighty traveller when on holiday; Member of Parliament at home.

John Ball already had a considerable knowledge of the whole Alpine chain, for by 1863 he was able to say he had crossed over 130 passes. But he was never the "scrambler" in the Whymper manner. Only three major peaks were first ascended by him, and all are in the Dolomites—Monte Pelmo, Marmolata di Rocca, Cima Tosa. Even the latter was later found to be second to an Italian ascent of which he was unaware. Not until after his death, when his diaries were made public, did any detailed account of his ascents appear.

Pelmo is a massive peak, made up of a series of very steep buttresses, leading to a plateau. Above this stretches a rock ridge to the summit. In 1857 four routes to the plateau were known to a few of the more hardy chamois hunters of the Val di Zoldo, among whom was numbered the parish priest! However, it was not he but another who was engaged by Ball to show the way. The atmosphere of the period and manner of the climb are best left to shine through the short notes of the diary:

Borca. 19.9.1857.

"... Started in time to hear 3 a.m., on the bridge. About 4 saw a bright fire on the rocks of the Anteleo high up, a hunter. Soon after Venus rose behind a rock so bright as to throw a decided shadow. Jupiter overhead. Dawn approached and grew as we reached the casera. At 5 we waited hearly half an hour while I screwed in points to my boots in the hut....

"Sun rose, and soon reached us as we left the ridge forming the pass to Zoppé to ascend the outer buttress that springs against the rocks of the Pelmo. You take the rocks just under the great tower which rises 5000 ft overhead, and after climbing some steep rocks with rubbed edges and shelves of debris you get on the ledge which you are to follow for 1½ hr. You soon come to the place which my guide expected was to turn me back. Three successive bays are passed, tolerable footing except here and there. The third is the *pons asinorum.* The rock projects leaving the shelf but 1½ ft high. The guide went forward to see how the land lay. After a few minutes he returned saying it was impossible to pass ... before giving it up I said I would look, and I found that I could pass, which I did, leaving one leg outside to catch the edges.

> "Here the real ascent begins . . . at first tolerably easy but after some rocks with plants on the ledges you take to the debris, very long and fatiguing. Snow leads to the last debris, and finally a small platform. The guide told me that that was as far as we could go, and on my pointing to a ridge terminating in a rock 80 or 100 ft higher he said there was no use going there as the view was interrupted by a higher and inaccessible point. I said let us go there at all events . . . the guide implored me to desist. . . . With a little caution in passing from one jagged and rotten tooth to another I gained the ridge, easy and safe, about 200 yds long. Top exactly at one."

Again, as on the famous passage of the Schwarztor in 1845, Ball led on when his "guide" lost courage.

In a later visit, in 1860, Ball attempted the Marmolata from the northern side, reaching a high point of the ridge towards Rocca but short of the main summit. He left a thermometer on the rocks, which was recovered in 1862 by Paul Grohmann, the famous Austrian explorer of the region, who has, of course, more summits to his credit than John Ball.

In later years Grohmann extended the work. Around Cortina, the Antelao and Tofana di Mezzo were climbed by him in 1863; Tofana di Rozes and Sorapiss in 1864; Monte Cristallo, Tofana di Fuori, and the Croda Rossa in 1865. In 1869 he ascended the Dreischusterspitze. Included in his work in the Western Dolomites we note particularly the ascent of the Langkofel in the same year.

But the collective English contribution to the general as well as the mountain exploration of the Dolomites was considerable. These mountains and valleys inspired one of the finest books of travel that has ever been written, *The Dolomite Mountains*, by Josiah Gilbert and G. C. Churchill. Of Gilbert it was said that "he probably never climbed what is called a difficult mountain in his life". Nevertheless he was an Alpine pioneer in the best sense of the word, and "his name and presence among us [the Alpine Club] have been for many years valuable in helping to keep and prove the Club true to its original broad aim and purpose as a body with brains as well as limbs". He was by profession a portrait painter, and his skill as an artist was the foundation of both the chromo-lithographs and the wood-engravings in the book.

Churchill was a solicitor, and apparently a good one, for by 1863, when he was forty-one, he was able to retire and devote himself to the botanical and geological studies that were his devotion. His knowledge of such matters was considered second only to that of John Ball.

The partners had already seen the Dolomites as early as 1856, but not until 1861–3 did they thoroughly explore the valleys of the region and make some pass walks. The combination was a fine one, and the publication of their book in 1864 was warmly received by the English travelling public:

> "The new mountains introduced to the Alpine Society were speedily adopted into mountaineers' favour. Mr Ball proved one of their most enthusiastic devotees; Mr Leslie Stephen a respectful, Mr Tuckett an assiduous, and Mr Holzmann a laborious worshipper. The Pelmo and the Cimon della Pala became household words, and it was generally admitted, even among those who cared for mountains only for climbing's sake, that Dolomite climbs had a fine flavour of their own."

The book is one which no traveller among mountains today, above all no visitor to the region, can omit reading, nor can he follow without great pleasure the history and tales of human contacts that make the people of these mountains live again in the primitive atmosphere of nearly a century ago.

One omission may be noted—the Dolomites of the Brenta, west of the Adige, which in 1863 were described by John Ball in his travellers' guide, *The Central Alps*.

Ball's own work on the Dolomites was included with the whole of the Tyrolese and Bavarian highlands in his companion guide, *The Eastern Alps*, published in 1868.

Before the publication of Ball's guides other Englishmen, mainly climbers, had paid visits and made individual contributions to the exploration of the heights. Lord Francis Douglas, killed on the Matterhorn in the tragedy of 1865, had the previous year made the second ascent of the Antelao, and this was in fact the first Dolomite ascent to be noted in the *Alpine Journal* (Vol. 1).

Although published later (1876), Grohmann's *Wanderungen in den Dolomiten* was of more limited value than either Ball or Gilbert and Churchill. In spite of his detailed studies, he excluded from his pages large and important areas, *e.g.* the Brenta and Primiero districts, as well as the Marmolata, and dealt mainly with the Cortina and Sexten areas. Mr (afterwards Sir Maurice) Holzmann, a meticulous student and authority on the region covered by Grohmann, who had spent five years in exploration of the Cortina district, had much to criticise in his needless Germanisation of names. For instance, the Paternsattel instead of the Lavaredo Sattel, between the Paternkofel and the Drei Zinnen. In fact, the name of Lavaredo had become so neglected by the time the district was completely renamed by the Italians that many climbers of the last generation attributed the name to Mussolini and his minions, when it was really a reversion to an ancient form accepted by even the northern German-speaking peasants. In general, whatever the debt owed by mountaineers to Grohmann, his book is less deserving of note than the two English productions.

In the same year as Lord Francis Douglas' visit, John Ball crossed the Bocca di Brenta from Molveno to Pinzolo, finding on the Pinzolo side "a well beaten cattle track", whilst the approach from Molveno was well known to chamois hunters, one of whom, Bonifacio Nicolussi, led him there. It was in the following year, 1865, that Ball made his ascent of the Cima Tosa. In those days, from Pinzolo at least, it was known as the Brenta Alta, a name now given to the mass on the opposite side of the Bocca.

Artists and photographers were busy early. Only the year after Gilbert and Churchill (1865) appeared a folio of *Twenty-three Photographs of the Dolomite Mountains*, by W. D. Howard and F. H. Lloyd, whilst the short series of pen and wash drawings made by Elijah Walton (who was as accomplished an artist as Gilbert), in his tour of 1866, are among the most vivid representations of these mountains that have ever been achieved, even by the great E. T. Compton himself.

A worthy contemporary of John Ball, Francis Fox Tuckett, an early member and lifelong friend of the Austrian Alpine Club, was at work in the Dolomites in 1863. Approaching from Lienz, via Toblach and Landro, he visited Cortina, continuing the journey by the Falzarego Pass to Pieve d'Andraz. He then went with his party to Contrin under the Marmolata, then on to the Grödnerjoch, through the Rosengarten massif, and ended at Bozen.

He was there again in 1865 with friends J. H. Fox, D. W. Freshfield, and J. H. Backhouse, with the two Devouassouds, who were Chamonix guides. At first they did a little pass exploration at Primiero, then went over to the Marmolata for an early ascent by the Grohmann route over the northern slopes. Further pass walking followed, around Cortina. Later in the holiday Tuckett and Freshfield with the guides went to the Bocca di Brenta, with designs on the Cima Tosa, but were defeated by bad weather, as had been the case with Antelao a fortnight or so previously.

A visit in 1867 again disappointed him on the Antelao, which had too much snow, but he made up for this by the first ascent of Civetta, with his Swiss guides the Andereggs and a local guide. This was on May 31st, very early in the season even for the Dolomites. On June 6th he succeeded also in getting the Cima Tosa, with Anderegg and Bonifacio Nicolussi.

In 1869, among other expeditions, Tuckett made the second ascent of Monte Cristallo, with the first descent over the glacier to Schluderbach. This was with his friend E. Howard, the guides being Christian Lauener and Santo Siorpaes. Defeated by weather on the Tofana, he made another ascent of the Marmolata with the same party plus J. H. Fox (who was later lost in the Caucasus with Donkin).

In 1870 his companion was E. R. Whitwell, and he again engaged both Lauener and Siorpaes. The Monte Pavione was crossed from Feltre to Primiero: on May 27th the first attempt to climb the virgin Cimon della Pala was made, but only the *Vorgipfel* was reached. Whitwell attempted the Pala di San Martino, whilst Tuckett alone climbed the Cima di Fradusta. The Cimon della Pala was actually ascended by Whitwell and the guides on June 1st, Tuckett not being fit enough to join them.

[Incidentally, the second and third ascents of the Cimon della Pala in August and September 1876 are interesting. It was very appropriate that the local landowner, Count Welsberg himself, with Albert de Falkner, a well-known Italian explorer of the Brenta, accompanied by five guides under the leadership of Santo Siorpaes, achieved the second. The third ascent, again with Santo Siorpaes, was by W. A. B. Coolidge, the Alpine historian, shortly afterwards, and this ascent was one of the reasons for his irony quoted previously on page 68.]

Whitwell continued this successful tour by climbing Piz Popena on June 16th, and the Croda Rossa on June 20th. At last, the third effort, Tuckett with the party got Antelao on June 18th. Still not fit enough for the Croda Rossa, he left his friends to make the first ascent whilst he climbed the much duller Tofana with two local guides. After other wanderings the party reached the Langkofel ridge, but not the summit, on August 12th, being driven off in hail and thunder.

In 1872 he was again in the Dolomites with the guides Lauener and Siorpaes. After missing Pelmo on June 15th, he made a new route up the Marmolata by the Marmolatascharte on June 17th, following the west arête and the descent to Fedaia, thus making the first complete traverse of this highest of all the peaks. June 18th was the day for the Plattkofel, and June 19th he walked through the Rosengarten, where the scenery impressed him considerably. It was a result of this day's reconnaissance that enabled him to pass on to two other Englishmen the information which they used to make the first ascent in August of the highest peak, the Kesselkogel (Catinaccio d'Antermoia), which fits into the pattern a little later.

The third great pioneer, after Ball and Tuckett, was Leslie Stephen. His paper to the Alpine Club, *The Peaks of Primiero*, read on January 25th, 1870, is one of the masterpieces of mountaineering prose. Walking from Primiero via Castel Pietra into the Val di Canali, he described the superb scenery there to be found.

Passing from this valley into the middle of the great cirque of peaks, he climbed the nameless summit which was later known as the Cima di Ball, in honour of John Ball. A few days after this ascent, again alone, Stephen climbed the Fradusta, noting as he travelled, the tremendous sweep of the Sass Maor and of the Pala, which had recently defeated even Grohmann.

By 1870, therefore, the district was being thoroughly opened up. Santo Siorpaes and Angelo Dimai, excellent Cortina men, were often Grohmann's guides, and also supplemented the Swiss guides at times brought out by English mountaineers. Other peaks began to fall. 1872 was a very good year: not only was Tuckett's new route made up the Marmolata, and repeated by another English party a fortnight later, but the Becco di Mezzodi was conquered by Utterson Kelso again with Siorpaes; the second ascent of the Langkofel was made by the same party, and also the first ascent of the Marmarole, whilst C. C. Tucker with Bernard of Campitello climbed the Kesselkogel. Lastly, in September of the year, Tucker, with D. W. Freshfield, climbed the Cima di Vezzana via the Travignolo glacier. This was thought to be lower than the Cimon, but in fact it was the highest of all the Primiero peaks.

Although strict chronology places the exploration of the Brenta in the second or rock-climbing period, it is best to include it as a belated part of the pioneering age. The greatest individual contribution to the opening up of the Brenta peaks (apart from the early ascents of Tosa and Brenta) was the determined and comprehensive onslaughts in 1882–4 of another Englishman, Edward Theodore Compton, with his friend Albert de Falkner and the guide Nicolussi. The party climbed the Torre di Brenta, Cima Brenta Bassa, the Brenta Alta, the Crozzon di Brenta by the ridge, the Pietra Grande, the western Cima Ceda, the Punta di Campiglio, the Cima Sella, and the Cima Molveno—one of the most concentrated and impressive lists that any pioneer could produce.

Compton's explorations were embodied in important papers to the Alpine Club and to the foreign clubs. His map and line sketches of the range considerably clarified knowledge of their topography and interrelationship at a time when the Austrian military maps were very poor and other independent surveys had not been made. Compton was of course an accomplished draughtsman and artist of the naturalistic "Munich" school, where he studied. He lived all his life in Bavaria, and the combination of climbing skill with artistic talent made him the most famous painter and illustrator of mountains "for mountaineers" who has ever lived.

EARLY GUIDES

The early climbers were really the chamois hunters. Freshfield praises the Italians of the Val di Zoldo: "Where else in the Alps will he find a valley, the natives of which alone, and untainted by foreign gold, have found their way to the tops of the highest peaks?"

But in general their knowledge stopped at the highest plateaux where chamois were likely to go, and did not include the steeper glaciers and upper crags, where their English employers, or their imported Swiss guides, often led the way. But of many climbs it could be said, as Kugy did of his route on Triglav, "*first ascent (or descent) by anyone* not *carrying a chamois*".

I have spoken of the English achievement, and the expression is just. It really was achievement, and not merely the hiring and following of a skilled guide. The planning, the hour-to-hour tactics, the inspiration were theirs, even with good men. But so many of the early ascents were with men who fell short of the Val di Zoldo standard, and whose general opinion was that "this going ware glory waits ye h'ain't one agreeable feetur". Ball had trouble with his guide on the Tosa; Tucker and Freshfield actually dismissed their man, who was afraid of the ice at the foot of the Travignolo glacier, and ascended the Vezzana themselves. Stephen crisply summed up his early guide, Rosso Colesel: "Colesel is very poor and very deserving. He is willing, exceedingly cheerful, full of conversation which I regret to say was imperfectly intelligible to his companion, a good walker and a mighty bearer of weights. In short he has every virtue a guide can have consistently with a total and profound ignorance of the whole theory and practice of mountain climbing."

C. C. Tucker and Carson on the Kesselkogel in 1872 took effective steps to handle a problem guide: "We quickly uncoiled and put on the rope, the guide, who looked extremely blue but made no remonstrance, being securely tied *between us* with a double knot."

Above a mass of inferiors towered the great Santo Siorpaes, guide and friend of every climber of distinction in the Dolomite region during this period. When he was not available they were conscious of the gap. Tucker himself, on the same holiday of 1872, complains: "We were met by the unwelcome news that Santo Siorpaes, to whose skill we had trusted for the realisation of many shadowy plans, was away from home travelling with an English lady in Switzerland or Italy. This proceeding on the part of the English lady we resented much; to take a Tyrolese guide to Switzerland was, we argued, to carry coals to Newcastle; to take him to Italy was to put him where he could be no sort of use to anybody."

The English lady concerned is soon identified, for in her book *Untrodden Peaks and Unfrequented Valleys*, Miss Amelia Edwards, the spirited traveller herself, says of him, "a brave, hardy, faithful fellow who travelled with us later in the autumn of [1872] among the Italian Alps and through the Zermatt district". She gives us also those few personal impressions that bring him to life, "a bright-eyed, black-haired mountaineer of about forty; a mighty chamois hunter; an ex-soldier in the Austrian army, and now a custodian of forests and local inspector of roads. An active eager fellow brown as a berry with honesty written on his face. . . ."

* * * *

The twenty years from 1857 to 1877 cover the early mountain period, where easy ways were sought, the major summits achieved, and the district established as a climbing centre. Remarkable developments followed in the next period, when the hundreds of minor peaks and pinnacles were climbed, and new routes made on the big peaks. In the latter years of the period some amazing feats of severe rock work were carried through and this part of the Tyrol firmly established as worthy to rank level as a rock-climbing area with even the Aiguilles of Chamonix.

ROCK-CLIMBING (FIRST PERIOD)

Perhaps a suitable landmark of the beginning of the rock-climbing period was the ascent by C. C. Tucker in 1875 of the Sass Maor, a very difficult pinnacle but one of distinctly inferior height, and not among the three-thousand-metre peaks that the old pioneers had exclusively ascended. This age of development during the twenty-five years to the end of the century was marked by three distinctive features:

First, the rapid growth of the Deutscher und Oesterreichischer Alpenverein, formed in 1874 from the German and the Austrian Clubs, and of the Societa degli Alpinisti Tridentini, formed in 1873 (now a section of the Club Alpino Italiano but in those days much more important in the Brenta and Western Dolomites than the C.A.I.). This growth of club membership, with its concomitant growth of funds, enabled the clubs to build many Alpine huts at convenient valley heads and among the wildest glens of the peaks, and so give a great impetus to further explorations, especially for week-end parties. Moreover, both clubs were open to a wider range of climbers than the exclusive English club of the period.

Secondly, the great activity of German and Austrian guideless climbers, especially Ludwig Purtscheller and the Brothers Zsigmondy, whose skill and vigour of approach set new standards, and whose tendency to develop a local type of climbing, instead of a mere adaptation of the cautious guided and traditional style that preceded it, led to many brilliant ascents. It also led to a large and disturbing number of deaths, particularly among solitary climbers, who were numerous by comparison with those in Switzerland.

Thirdly, a parallel and significant development was the emergence of an adequate corps of good guides, under the steady patronage of foreign (*i.e.* English) climbers. Whilst the good men of the earlier age were, as we have seen, very few, by the 'nineties every valley had its group of guides, expert at their own crags, though often inclined to be lost outside the Dolomites. At Cortina there were the Siorpaes, the Dimais, the Verzis; in Fassa the Bernards; at Primiero the Bettegas and Zagonels; in the Brenta the Nicolussis and Alimontas; and perhaps greatest of all, the Innerkoflers of Sexten.

Of Michel Innerkofler we have an early impression by Mr W. A. Baillie-Grohmann:

> "My special crony in those days was a young native of the Sextenthal. and I doubt if there ever were two happier climbing comrades, scrambling about from dawn to dusk, backing each other up desperate-looking chimneys and crawling across impossible-looking perpendicular cliffs, than were Michel Innerkofler and the writer. Michel became afterwards the most noted guide in the Schluderbach region, but at this time he was a humble *knecht* at old Ploner's mountain inn, and he went with me for a

> wage of a florin and a half, not as a guide, but as a brother mountaineer. We shared our loads, slept out in haylofts under one blanket, and helped each other over giddy *mauvais pas* . . . we hardly ever used the rope. . . ."

Michel Innerkofler, before his death in the crevasses of the Cristallo glacier in 1888 when he was only forty, had solved the two last problems of the big peaks—the Zwölferkofel in 1875, the Elferkofel in 1878. The Kleine Zinne (Cima Piccola di Lavaredo), the hardest "gymnastic" route of its day, was climbed by him in 1881, and in the same year with his brother Johann he led Diamantidi over all three summits of Lavaredo in one day. In 1880 he made a solitary ascent of the Grohmannspitze.

Among distinguished Austrian or Tyrolese amateurs were Robert Hans Schmitt and Johann Santner, whose best known first ascent was of the Fünffingerspitze by the Schmittkamin in 1890. Ludwig Norman-Neruda made the even more famous "competitive" ascent from the north two years later. Previously Schmitt had many ascents in the Rosengarten and Latemar to his credit. Santner, alone, climbed in 1880 the pinnacle of the Schlern that bears his name, whilst other solitary ascents were of the Mittel Grasleitenspitze, the Fallwand, and the West Kesselkogel.

Bernard of Campitello was a good guide of the period, climbing with such men as Merzbacher, Euringer, and Darmstadter. With Merzbacher he made the ascent of the Grand Vernel in 1879, and in 1881 the conquest of the first of the six Vajolet towers; with Euringer the pinnacle of the Schlern, later known as the Euringerspitze; and also the highest point of the Latemar. With Darmstadter he discovered the (now) standard route up the Cimon della Pala, which is better than the old stone-swept route. In this 1889 expedition he was joined by his fellow guide Stabeler, from his own valley, who also achieved distinction by climbing in 1892 the central Vajolet tower that carries his name (Plate 139), and also the east and north towers in the same year. The more difficult Winkler Tower had been climbed in 1887 by the phenomenal Georg Winkler, another young Austrian whose earliest triumph at the age of sixteen had been the Cima della Madonna at Primiero by the Winkler Kamrin. His climb of the Winkler Tower was made alone. The terrific Delago, most exposed of the three, waited until 1895. It was left to Hans Barth and E. Pichl in 1899 to make the traverse of all three towers in a day, and the famous overhanging chimney that has to be overcome on this traverse is rightly named the Pichlriss (Plate 138).

One by one the inaccessible towers had been falling since the Sass Maor in 1875, until last, and perhaps best of all, that fantastic obelisk the Guglia di Brenta was climbed in 1899. The greater part of the route, in fact to within about 150 feet of the summit, had been successfully explored and then descended by a party of Trentine climbers two years previously, Carlo Gabari with a Primiero guide named Tavernaro and a porter, Pooli. The hardest pitch of the climb, the Pooli wall near the start, is named after this porter. These climbers, for some reason, never resumed the attack, and it was left to two young Innsbruck students, Otto Ampferer and Karl Berger, to complete the climb by an exposed twenty-five-foot traverse from the "terrazzino Gabari" to the appalling north wall, where a hundred-foot-pitch with small holds was the clue to the ascent, for after this section only easier rocks remained.

With this splendid success we may usefully close this second stage of summit conquests, the first rock gymnastics era, though the dividing line is necessarily artificial, for some minor pinnacles remained unconquered until the twentieth century.

ROCK-CLIMBING (MODERN PERIOD)

In the twentieth century the predominant phase was that of the variation climb, the deliberately chosen difficult wall or rib, for the purpose of making a first-rate approach to an already accessible summit—essentially the designing of routes affording elegant work. Only a few climbs can be mentioned of the hundreds made. A high place is held by the first of this type of climb made in 1901, when two San Martino guides, Bettega and Zagonel, led Miss Beatrice Thomasson up the South Wall of the Marmolata, still one of the finest climbs in the region.

Again the guides and the Austrians share the honours, in general. Rudolph Fehrmann discovered his impressive route from the south up the Guglia in 1907, and a north wall of similar exposure on the Kleine Zinne in 1909. In 1905 the rib or arête of the Crozzon di Brenta had been traced by the Austrians, a three-thousand-foot climb of great distinction.

Face routes were done on the Langkofel, in the Rosengarten, and indeed everywhere. Among the most notable personal achievements was the solitary climb of nearly a thousand feet by Paul Preuss in 1911 up the Guglia East Wall, of which the last half was new.

Dr Preuss, an Austrian, was the most outstanding of the guideless and solitary climbers of his generation, as Emil Zsigmondy had been of his day. In men of this calibre the sheer love of climbing burned like a flame, and impelled them to achievements that few can, or would wish to, emulate. Preuss was particularly successful as a solitary climber, and his attack upon the upper East Wall of the Guglia di Brenta was a matchless effort of the will. Among his other achievements were the first (again solitary) ascent of Kleinste Zinne, the north-east face of the Crozzon di Brenta, and the South Wall of the Innerkoflerthurm. As an example of sustained nerve and physical endurance, his solitary traverse in one day of the Langkofel, Fünffingerspitze, and Grohmannspitze has never been surpassed. A man of considerable intellectual power, he wrote and spoke much of the mountain lands to which he was so devoted, and he was a firm supporter of "straight" climbing, almost in the English style, contending that artificial aids were justifiable only in case of emergency, and that pitons as well as ropes were not to be made the basis of a system of mountaineering. Like Zsigmondy, who was killed in the Alps at twenty-four, Preuss died young. He was only twenty-seven when he fell from the North Wall of the Mandlwand in October 1913.

The more extensive use of pitons had already begun in the Kaisergebirge and similar limestone districts, from which it was later to spread to the Dolomites. So little was even the technique of piton belays known among earlier English visitors that Broome remarks of his 1906 ascent of the Marmolata South Wall: "From time to time we saw small pitons, which were, of course, *useless for ascending*, so could only be supposed to have been fixed by a former party with a view to possible descent."

But it was still a far cry, in these early tentatives, to the full-scale haulage of the more remarkable sixth-grade climbs in the ten years of mountaineering that preceded the last war.

In the 1900's Englishmen still came to the Dolomites and, though climbing with guides, gave a good account of themselves. Mr E. A. Broome, with his parties, was perhaps the best known and of whom we have the fullest record. Mr Meade, with his Dauphiné guide Pierre Blanc, achieved fame by getting lost on the Guglia in following a route marked by two pitons which, unknown to them, had been inserted by an Austrian who had fallen immediately afterwards. But Blanc led brilliantly and a new variation was achieved. Though pitons were used in those days, the convenient karabiner or clip-ring had not been invented, so that it was necessary for Mr Meade to unrope and re-thread at the pitons—a dangerous and nerve-racking procedure that today is unnecessary.

The work of Austrian guideless climbers of the period, comparable with that of the many fine climbers who were quite independently developing British cragsmanship, was a feature of the 1900–14 generation as of the previous two decades. So was the work of the *guides d'élite*, who made a great contribution to the opening of new and elegant routes. At the turn of the century Antonio Dimai and Agostino Verzi were probably the best team, with the great Sepp Innerkofler as their chief rival.

Innerkofler was a remarkably fine type of Tyrolese from the Sexten glen and a member of a famous family of guides. Although he was over fifty when war broke out in 1915, he joined the *Jäger* with his two boys of eighteen and twenty-two. He was killed in a very gallant attack on an Italian outpost. It became necessary to attack an observation post on the Paternkofel, and with five other guides Innerkofler volunteered to try the hazardous job of climbing the north-east ridge before sunrise and attacking from the top of the steep final chimney. The climb was successfully done, but his grenades failed to explode and he was shot by the Italians who counter-attacked.* His body fell into the chimney, from which it was recovered and buried on the small summit plateau by the Italians with military honours. Three years later his sons, with a military patrol, recovered the body and carried it to his native valley of Sexten.

Of the guides before the Great War two others deserve special mention. The first is Angelo Dibona, whose name calls to mind many exposed routes such as the North Face of the Einserkofel, and the South Rib of the Croz dell'Altissimo, a thousand-metre climb in the Brenta. He was among the few men whose employers took him to the greater peaks to the west. Dibona (mainly with Dr Hans Mayer) climbed in the Swiss Alps and Chamonix Aiguilles, where a distinctive route on the face of the Requin was led by him; and his craftmark is also known in wild Dauphiné.

A point often overlooked by the critics of the Dolomite gymnasts is that it was often lack of opportunity rather than merely specialised skill on rock that prevented them from making ascents of distinction in the high Alps. The Austrian amateurs, from Purtscheller and Zsigmondy onwards, like such guides as Dibona, could give a very good account of themselves when they tried.

Another famous guide was Giovanni Battista Piaz, "*il diavolo delle Dolomiti*", as an old Campiglio guide once described him to me. Piaz really *was* one of the

* So runs the official account. I was talking of this in Aug. 1950 to his son Sepp II, who told me that his father was shot in the back by an Austrian machine gunner from the Innicher Riedel as his silhouette appeared against the sky at the summit.

specialised gymnastic types of the years before the war. He was, in some ways, to that age what Comici was to the 'thirties (page 84). He made some remarkable climbs, though they were often mere stunts like his traverse of the Vajolet Towers on a moonless night, or his throwing the rope over the Guglia di Amicis. He had one of the earliest motor-cycles and was not without means, so that he was really an "amateur" guide, climbing with whom he chose. He became a friend of Guido Rey, who perhaps praises him a little too fulsomely. The other extreme, showing complete lack of sympathy, is shown in the comments of Colonel Strutt, an enthusiastic climber in Tyrol but above all a devoted friend of everything Austrian. (Incidentally, Strutt was the man who safely escorted the Austrian Royal Family over the Swiss border after the Great War.) He has said that for undiluted arrogance and conceit without limit Piaz was unique—Maximin Gaspard and a certain Chamonix guide must appear modest compared with him. Whilst Piaz had a few sound new routes to his credit, he was never the equal of a Dimai or a Dibona. Colonel Strutt certainly had a far better impression of Antonio Dimai, a guide of his youth. He tells a charming story of their meeting at Cortina in 1933, when Dimai was seventy. The boring speeches of an Alpine Conference proving too much for them, these veteran climbers, employer and guide, went off to the Tre Cime to climb the Grosse Zinne, as friends for old time's sake, meeting as they descended two youths who had just made, with a bivouac, the third ascent of the North Wall by the piton route.

Even the Great War yielded additions to the climbing records, the first descent of the South Wall of the Marmolata by an Italian patrol in 1916, and the first ascent of the Marmolata di Rocca by the South Wall.

[The training of mountain troops both in Italy and Germany was largely guided by the experiences on these mountain frontiers; among many remarkable feats by Alpini, a few years before the recent war, was the haulage of machine-guns to the top of the Guglia di Brenta.]

After the war there followed the transfer of the district to Italy, the handing over of such huts as had survived to the Italian Alpine Club, which took in the Trentine Alpine Society and the local sections (Ampezzo, Bozen, etc.) of the D. & Oe. A.V.

There was an immediate recession of Austrian and especially German visits, and an increased activity by Italians in what had for so long been not only *Italia Irredenta* but a fortified frontier region.

Nevertheless, a few more problems were invented by Austrians, notably the

29. Monte Pelmo, after Elijah Walton, 1866 (the first Dolomite peak ascended; by John Ball, first President of the Alpine Club)

130. Modern Climbing Equipment: Kletterschuhe, Rope Sling, Pitons, Karabiners, Piton Hammer
131. Rifugio Locatelli, with North Face routes of the Cime di Lavaredo (see page 90 for details)

32. An Easy Rock Ridge (Cimon della Pala)

133. A Difficult Rock Face (South Wall of the Castelletto Inferiore, Brenta)

134. Climbing the Sella Towers (set of three)

135. The Sella Towers in line

136. The Vajolet Towers from below.

137
Pichlriss
on Delago

138
Stabeler
from Winkler

139
Climbing
on the Winkler
Tower

140
The
Summit of
Winkler

141. Grohmannspitze and Fünffingerspitze

42. A young Italian Guide (G. Alimonta on the summit of the Guglia di Brenta)

143. An old Tyrolese Guide (Michel Innerkofler III of Sexten, nephew of the great Sepp. Innerkofler)

144. Fifth Grade (an overhang with considerable exposure: pitons used as safeguards)

145. A Dolomite *Grande Course*: the Marmolata South Wall

46. Demetz on the Wall

147. Traverse to the First Terrace of the Wall

148. Nearing the Summit of the Climb
149. The Summit Ridge of the Marmolata

150. Roping down (Cima della Madonna, Primiero)

Schleierkante, the fine "outside edge" route of the Cima della Madonna (1920), and the Steger route of the Einser North Wall (1928).

But the Italian tide was flowing in on a broad front.

MECHANISED CLIMBING

The improvement of cheap transport, the democratisation of the sport which had been foreshadowed even before the war, all aided this wider popularity. The use of pitons as hand or footholds, and clip-rings as aids to haulage, created a special style of "mechanised" climbing and led to a different approach if not always to a higher standard of achievement.

The new system of grading was introduced, with climbs classified from I to VI.

In so far as comparisons are possible, the details below may help to give an idea of the grades, compared with well-known British climbs and some Alpine climbs:

Dolomite	*Alpine*	*British*
	GRADE I	
Cima Brenta (ordinary route)	Stockhorn, Zermatt	Snowdon Horseshoe or Skye Ridges
	GRADE II	
Cimon della Pala (ordinary route)	Wetterhorn (ordinary route)	Tower Ridge of Ben Nevis in summer
	GRADE III	
Stabeler (Vajolet Towers)	Aiguille de l'M, Chamonix	Grooved Arête of Tryfan
Cima Grande di Lavaredo (ordinary route)	Wellenkuppe	
Langkofel (Felsen route)	Zinal Rothorn	North or New West climbs on Pillar Rock
	GRADE IV	
Winkler Tower	Aiguille de Grépon (ordinary way)	Pillar, North-West Climb
Cinque Dita (Schmitt)	Dent du Géant (North Wall)	Longland's Climb, Clogwyn du'r Arddu
Marmolata South Wall		
	GRADE V	
Guglia di Brenta	Face of Dent du Requin	Pigott's Climb, Clogwyn du'r Arddu
North Wall of Einserkofel	Mer de Glace face, Grépon	Central Buttress, Scafell

I repeat: *so far as comparisons are possible*—here they are not possible:

	GRADE VI	
Spigolo Giallo Kleine Zinne	North Wall of Matterhorn	None
North Wall of Grosse Zinne	Eigerwand	

Grade I is almost a cattle track, Grade IV perhaps represents the limit of human effort as it was before 1900, whilst Grade V is that which includes climbs offering the most extreme difficulty capable of being overcome without the use of pitons as climbing aids, though pitons are used for belays.

The Grade VI is reserved for ascents in the new manner. It was a natural development among these limestone crags, so well adapted in their formation to the use of such methods, and with enough rock and to spare for those who found and find mechanised climbing to be objectionable. Many parties were characterised by extreme youth, by desperate recklessness rather than cold skill, and also by the inordinate length of time they took to do their routes, which were not always well designed. The new method suffered much in the estimation of experienced climbers, from orthodox prejudice, from its high death roll, and from the political cast given to such work both by the German and Italian rulers. It was urged on not so much by kicks as by carrots: "The medal for valour in sport will be awarded to climbers who make new ascents of the sixth grade" (Mussolini).

Naturally, stunts were indulged in. An enormous length of ropes and large numbers of pitons were used by Comici and his fellow-guides when they made perhaps the most spectacular "steeplejack" climb ever done, up the vertical North Wall of the Grosse Zinne. Yet even that has settled down today into an affair of a mere 50 pitons—not as bad as was originally thought. And, pitons or no pitons, the later ascent of this climb by Comici *alone*, ranks as one of the most daring achievements on record.

These dangerous or excessively fancy climbs have received most publicity, but for the modern experts the sixth-grade climb has come to stay. It is the only method still yielding fine long climbs in the Dolomites for those to whom a "first ascent" matters more, as a sporting achievement, than any other type of climb. Even the narrow superficial area of the slender Guglia di Brenta, which one would have thought variated out of existence long ago, has yielded, as recently as August 1947, a fine "outside edge" climb in the new style, 370 metres in length and taking for those first making the route no less than 19 hours. This is by no means the longest time taken—a Grade VI (the Via Oppia) on the Croz dell'Altissimo took 84 hours (three bivouacs). This climb was not repeated until July 1949, ten years after the first ascent.

No doubt there will in time be a seventh grade, but the school of mountaineers who aver that from every struggle comes something that makes an even greater struggle necessary does not find me among their number. Nor, on the other hand, am I prepared to sigh overlong for the days of a century ago, when all was there to be done for the first time. This is a personal view. Climbing progresses, and every spearhead must have its tip. I speak from half-way down the shaft. Today, the sound climber of any degree of skill who has no ambitions as a "modern" is the real inheritor of a vast treasure-house of good routes to follow and enjoy.

* * * *

Apart from the development of the *sesto grado*, little had been left for the new tenants of the Dolomites to do, since the old owners had so comprehensively opened up the mountain ways.

Yet in that little remaining, the Italians did well. The huts which had been burned or shelled in the war were rebuilt and new ones added. Best of all, in the twenty years that followed, a magnificent series of guidebooks (*see* page 97) was produced under the care of the Italian Alpine Club. They are accurately detailed, giving much historical information and are equipped with clear sketch plans of peaks, and maps of the immediate surroundings. It is for these things rather than for the last few desperate explorations that the gratitude of mountaineers of every country is due.

Dolomite Climbing Technique

DOLOMITE climbing is almost as specialised a part of rock-climbing as rock-climbing itself is of the wider craft of mountaineering.

A great deal of nonsense has been talked about the Dolomites by some climbers, especially those trained for and attracted to the snow and ice peaks. Dolomites as peaks, it has been said, are contemptible. Certainly they are small in comparison with the great Swiss ice peaks or with Mont Blanc. The amount of ice work they offer is trivial, and often avoidable. The only glacier of any size, on the north slope of the Marmolata, is at an easy angle, and an almost uncrevassed route down from the summit to its snout can be found. Other glaciers, such as that on the north face of the Cristallo, are a little more tricky but, again, small. In late summer such old snow slopes as have survived wear a rather tired and dusty look.

The rock, however, is simply made to be climbed. Unlike even the British hills, which are of the tough volcanic rock alone capable of surviving the ice cap that once lay over them, the Dolomites have never been glaciated, and the rock is never smoothed to the extent that is seen elsewhere. Thus there is usually no lack of hand-and-foot hold (or at least finger-and-toe hold!), but the distinctive feature of all dolomite for the climber is the uncompromising exposure. Sheer verticality, often spoken of, is rarely encountered in the granite peaks, whilst in the Dolomites it is the type. There is no margin of safety for clumsy or careless climbers—balance and neatness are absolutely essential. Firm nerves are indispensable in the leader, and are also an advantage and comfort in and to those who follow.

A second feature of the rock is the stratified formation by which a series of short walls with little terraces, wide and narrow, build up a face. The Brenta range shows this with especial prominence, but it occurs often elsewhere, such as on the Vajolet Towers of the Rosengarten, on the Cime di Lavaredo, and best of all on Monte Pelmo. Remarkable traverses can be made along these "bands" which add to the complexities of route-finding.

The rock in its detail is hard and inclined to be brittle. It varies from a very rough, whitish or grey type to the yellow or reddish types which are smoother and less dependable. The redder tints are the signal for especial caution.

The earlier climbers frequently drew attention to its rottenness in general, but this does not apply to the standard routes, where previous parties have dislodged the more obvious loose holds, nor to the steep walls of modern harder climbs where little loose rock can adhere. Even so, there is always some stonefall with large parties and so it is best not to follow a route already occupied by climbers ahead.

In the main, since even the steep rock abounds in holds small but usable, a general line set by a pioneer can usually be followed along a broad front, a yard or more either left or right often being equally acceptable. In this it differs from most British and many Alpine rock faces. For instance, on such a traverse as that of the Grépon there is little alternative at such close range.

Dolomite rock shows either the vertical cliff with a flat-topped summit and an easy backstairs of slab and scree, or else the astonishingly slender pinnacle. Buttresses of peaks where seen at all are broad-walled, and the knife-edge rib is rare. One does not see arêtes comparable with those formed of granite or gneiss, of which it may be said that they are "vertical on one side and overhanging on the other". But dolomite has no lack of overhangs, and a large number of them are climbable.

If dolomite has few arêtes, it has many superb chimneys and gullies. This is particularly so where underlying volcanic disturbance appears to have cloven the limestone vertically. But the chimney formation is everywhere, and once the normal summit explorations had been made, new routes and rock climbs of the 'eighties and 'nineties were frequently made by these chimneys. Outstanding examples are the Schmitt-Kamin of the Fünffingerspitze, the Adang-Kamin of the Tschierspitze, and the Pichlriss of the Delagoturm.

* * * *

Equipment for climbing is much the same as in England or the Alps, with one important difference. Whereas at home and on snow peaks alike nailed boots are the normal wear because of the moss and mud likely to make soft soles slip, or the snow plods encountered, the usual wear in the Dolomites for many years has been felt-soled *kletterschuhe*. These soles are good when dry and very tenacious when wet. Nailed boots were of course used considerably in early exploration, and for the walking or scrambling to the foot of a climb. The habit grew up among guided parties, who were attacking the "wrong" side of a Dolomite, of employing a porter to take their boots at the foot of their route, ascend the mountain by the easiest available way, and place them at the summit. We hear of rope-soled shoes as early as 1875, when Bernard, a Campitello guide, made the first ascent of the slabby Gran Vernel in them; but the felted sole was not used until the 'nineties. In 1879 an English party on the Sass Maor used rubber tennis shoes, lending a pair to their guide, and spoke highly of them. It was in about the same period that Mummery used tennis shoes in the Alps.

One hears of the habit practised in England to this day of taking boots off when unexpected difficulty was met, such as on the first ascent of the Cimon della Pala by the Darmstadter route. Delago prospected his eponymous tower with bare feet. There is a very limited future for this type of sole in the Dolomites.

Today *kletterschuhe* and rubber tennis shoes are both used, but the almost universal wear for walkers and climbers is Vibram. These hard rubber soles stamped into the pattern of climbing nails are splendidly suited to the limestone, and all but the most difficult ascents can be made in them. I have done up to Grade IV without finding them too cumbersome but found that Grade V is a little more tricky than they can handle. Grade VI is outside their range (I presume). These soles were invented in Italy, and as long ago as 1937 I saw an Italian guide wearing them on the Dent du Géant, a difficult pinnacle on the French frontier of the Mont Blanc massif. Other equally good types of rubber sole are available, but the latest opinion in Italy is that Pirelli Alpina are the best.

An interesting compromise between normal *kletterschuhe* and heavy boots is to have Vibram soles, over a thin leather undersole, on *kletterschuhe* soft uppers.

* * * *

The long rope is absolutely essential in modern Dolomite climbing. Pitches (*i.e.* the distance between one belay and another) often run up a hundred feet, which is much longer vertically than horizontally, and the frequent need to abseil down a hard pitch makes length essential. The longest rope I have seen used was one of 175 feet on the Campanile Basso, and it was certainly needed on the descent, where one abseil was all of the 90 feet available on the double rope. The Italians generally favour the heavy hemp, but nylon, the new light rope, is being noticed by the experts, and such ropes are very soon snapped up if offered by visiting Englishmen.

* * * *

Because of the smallness of the glaciers snow goggles are hardly necessary unless a man is unduly subject to eyestrain. There is no danger of snow-blindness, or the burnt and blistered skins that make Alpine climbing such a trial at times. But a pair of the lightest Crookes tinted glasses is welcome on the white screes or among the occasional stretches of ice.

* * * *

Because of the general formation, with few spikes or bollards as seen on granite rocks, small ring-spikes (pitons, *mauerhaken*, *chiodi*) are often needed as belays or abseil points. From time to time there has been much loose talk about the Dolomites being ruined by these pitons as well as by the wire-cables, staircases, and iron stanchions. This is an exaggeration. True, the ordinary route up the Marmolata from Contrin is heavily decorated, but after all this is the normal route up the highest and therefore the most popular peak in the region.

There are other wire ropes here and there, mainly on popular peaks, but even so they are few, and there is nothing comparable with the appalling 250 metres of thick cable on the Mitteleegi ridge of the Eiger, the ropes and chains of the Géant, or even of the Matterhorn. Considering the volume of traffic, the Dolomite crags emerge from a charge of spoliation much more creditably than do many Swiss peaks.

The party on a normal climbing expedition will do well to carry a few pitons and a small hammer for the emergencies that can arise. Especially if bad weather comes suddenly, it may be essential to rope down immediately. Again, since there are no nail marks on the good rock climbs, a complicated route can easily be missed, and a few pitons may save lives.

* * * *

An ice-axe is generally an unnecessary encumbrance. One must be taken perhaps, for a party of three or four on the Marmolata or on the Cristallo glacier, and more on the Cima Tosa couloir, but otherwise there is no need for one in normal summer conditions. For the winter or early spring mountaineers matters are nearer to the Swiss standard, and an ice-axe per man is advisable.

* * * *

A feature of Dolomite climbs is their overall shortness—*i.e.* length of climb *plus* length of approach—by comparison with Swiss standards. There a start before sunrise is usually necessary, the party climbs hard against the insistent pressure of time, and it is often essential to be off the mountain as soon after noon as possible to avoid "buttery" glaciers and névé.

In the Dolomites the standards of comfort we are accustomed to in Wales or the English Lake District are more nearly approached. True, a big peak may demand a five-o'clock start, but generally seven or eight o'clock is early enough. Whilst for the rock climbs of average length, such as the Fünffingerspitze, a start nearer noon will still ensure a return before sunset.

This less exacting routine is largely possible because of the many excellent huts which cut out the hours of approach work otherwise involved.

* * * *

DETAILS OF PLATE 131

A. Cima Piccolissima (Kleinste Zinne)

B. Punta Frida

C. Cima Piccola (Kleine Zinne)

D. Cima Grande (Grosse Zinne)

Routes

1. *North-East Wall of Kleinste Zinne.* The famous Preuss route of 1911. Made entirely without the use of pitons, even as belays. A near-vertical and difficult climb. Grade V, 2 hours, approx. 700 ft.

2. *North Wall of Kleinste Zinne.* The Eckenstein–Rabanser route of 1948. A fully mechanised route, no less than 25 pitons being used. Grade VI superior, 11 hours, approx. 600 ft. new.

3. *Stosser–Schutt route* to a small col between Kleinste and Punta Frida at mid-height. Done in 1929. Grade V, some pitons used, 3 hours, approx. 450 ft.

4. *North Wall of Punta Frida.* The Dulfer–Piaz route made in 1912 by G. B. Piaz. Grade IV, 2 hours, approx. 450 ft.

5. *The Holzner route* of 1927. Difficult to follow, but of reasonable standard. Grade IV, 3½ hours, approx. 850 ft.

6. *The Grünwald–Siorpaes route* to the forcella between the Punta and Kleine Zinne. An old route of 1881, made by Santo Siorpaes. Grade II, ½ hour, approx. 700 ft.

7. *The North Wall of Kleine Zinne.* Made in 1890 by Sepp Innerkofler. The best standard route to the summit, a steep climb on sound rock. Grade IV, 2 hours, approx. 500 ft.

8. *The fine Fehrmann route* of 1909. A steep chimney route, seldom followed. 140 ft. rope needed. Grade V, 3 hours, approx. 1,000 ft.

9. *Spigolo Comici–Mazzorana.* An early mechanised route by the famous exponent of mechanised climbing, with his pupil, now the guardian of the Caldart hut. Numerous pitons, and two bivouacs! Grade VI superior, 2 days, approx. 1,000 ft.!

10. *The Phillimore route* to the Grosse Zinne. Made in 1897. Grade III, 4 hours, approx. 1,650 ft.

11. *Langl route* of 1911. Grade III, 4 hours, same length.

12. *A Langl variant.* Similar to above.

13. *The Spigolo Dibona.* A good, exposed route up the edge of the East Wall. Made by Angelo Dibona in 1909. Grade IV, 4 hours, approx. 1,800 ft.

14. *North Wall of Grosse Zinne.* The "Eigerwand" of the Eastern Alps. Made in 1933 by Comici and the Dimais, all guides, with great numbers of pitons and an enormous length of ropes. Has been repeated several times, and now said to carry about 50 pitons. The most remarkable achievement was Comici's *solitary* ascent. Grade VI superior, usually 2 days, approx. 1,800 ft.

15. *The Stosser route.* Another climb of extreme severity. Grade VI, 1 day, approx. 1,600 ft.

Conclusion

THE Dolomites are what you care to make them. To stick to the broad highway, white with limestone dust, and see over the green alps the great crags rising into the sky is but one way to travel. At the other extreme is the rarefied pursuit of the sixth grade for those who are so disposed. *Hunde! wollt ihr ewig leben?* might well be their war-cry to the passing motorists.

Middle courses have much merit. To tread the paths leading up into the high corries is pleasant and reasonably safe. Once there, comfort in a mountain inn can be enjoyed. Those who prefer a bivouac under the stars with a fire of pine boughs and a couch of bilberry or heather may pass the inn to seek little corries away from the huts.

Those who like to climb with guides can feel assured of competent professional help in any centre. Those who are skilled enough can justifiably do without a guide if they take care to select climbs which do not involve intricate route finding. The passing of the pioneering age, or of the first rock-climbing age, does not mean the routes are destroyed or worthless. We can mount the gentle slopes of the Marmolata glacier as Ball or Grohmann did; we can venture upon rock scrambles of any degree of difficulty, according to taste and ability.

Climbs can be short or long, we can go slow or fast as we choose, and I at least would say that of all the rock-climbing I have ever done, that of the Dolomites carries off the palm for thrills.

* * * *

At times there is much to be said for doing but little nor that little oft. We can laze in the hot sun, as Leslie Stephen did, under the chestnut trees above Primiero, and watch the changes in the aspect of the peaks.

It was in such a mood that, after eight consecutive days of hard climbing, I paid off my guide, and in a leisurely way went up by cool woodland paths to a green alp where I wandered at intervals over the meadows and along the fringes of the woods, content to enjoy the warm sun and the fresh beauty all around me. I saw few people—groups of haymakers; a peasant with his tiny cart; an occasional party of other walkers.

From the edge of a little pine-wood came voices singing in German, and I took the singers for a party of Tyrolese or Austrians. But they were a Roman lady and her children who turned to me, as they ended their song, with the friendly greetings that come so naturally to all Italians. After a little time in conversation, I asked them if they would sing again, and this time they gave one of those Alpini songs of the Great War—of such quality that all its poignancy was independent of the language. The blended voices sent out the cadences of the song sweet and clear over the broad alp, the summer breeze made shot-silk ripples over the hayfields, the blue cloud shadows drifted across the steep rock walls of the peaks, and among the shadows sparkled the grey-gold pinnacles as the sun caught them. It seemed already that such ethereal fantasies could never have been climbed, in war or in peace.

Yet in this book are photographs to remind us—in their grey ghostly way—that these lovely mountains are real, and that they wait to enchant anyone who can find a little leisure, a little money, and the patience to endure the journey across Europe.

Glossary of Austrian and Italian Names

(Principal names only)

Austrian Names	*Italian Names*
THE BRENNER ROUTE	THE BRENNER ROUTE
Etsch	Adige
Trent, Trient	Trento
Deutsch Metz	Mezzo Corona
Welsch Metz	Mezzo Lombardo
Eisak	Isarco
Bozen	Bolzano
Ritten	Renon
Mendel	La Mendola
Waidbruck	Ponte all'Isarco
Klausen	Chiusa
Talfer	Talvera
Brixen	Bressanone
Franzensfeste	Fortezza
PUSTERTHAL	VAL PUSTERIA
Bruneck	Brunico
Toblach	Dobbiaco
Innichen	San Candido
Sexten	Sesto
Prags	Braies
HÖHLENSTEINTHAL	VAL DI LANDRO
Dürrensee	Lago di Landro
Schluderbach	Carbonin
Peutelstein	Podestagno
GRÖDNERTHAL	VAL GARDENA
Kastelruth	Castelrotto
St Ulrich	Ortisei
St Christina	Santa Cristina
Wolkenstein	Selva
Grödnerjoch	Passo (di) Gardena

Glossary of Austrian and Italian Names

Austrian Names	*Italian Names*
ABTEITAL	VAL BADIA
Collfuschg	Colfosco
Stern	La Villa
St Leonhard	Badia
DOLOMITENSTRASSE	STRADA DOLOMITI
Eggenthal	Val d'Ega
Welschnofen	Nova Levante
Karersee	Carezza al Lago
Karer Pass	Passo di Costalunga
Buchenstein	Livinallongo

PRINCIPAL (3,000-METRE) PEAKS OF THE DOLOMITES

Austrian Name	*Italian Name*	*Metres*	*Feet*
Marmolata	Marmolada	3,342	10,965
Antelao	Antelao	3,263	10,706
Tofana	Tofana	3,243	10,640
Civetta	Civetta	3,218	10,558
Cristallospitze	Monte Cristallo	3,216	10,551
Sorapis	Sorapiss	3,205	10,515
Vernel	Gran Vernel	3,205	10,515
Cima di Vezzana	Cima di Vezzana	3,191	10,469
Cimon della Pala	Cimon della Pala	3,186	10,453
Langkofel	Sasso Lungo	3,181	10,436
Cima Tosa	Cima Tosa	3,173	10,410
Monte Pelmo	Monte Pelmo	3,168	10,394
Dreischusterspitze	Punta di Tre Scarperi	3,162	10,374
Piz Popena	Piz Popena	3,152	10,341
Boespitze	Piz Boé	3,151	10,338
Kaiser-Franz-Josef-Spitze	Cima Brenta	3,150	10,335
Hohe Gaisl	Croda Rossa	3,139	10,299
Grohmannspitze	Punta Grohmann	3,126	10,256
Zwölferkofel	Croda dei Toni, or Cima Dodici	3,094	10,151
Elferkofel	Cima Undici	3,092	10,145
Innerkoflerturm	Punta Innerkofler	3,072	10,079
Sasso Vernale	Sasso Vernale	3,054	10,020
Cima di Focobon	Cima di Focobon	3,054	10,020
Hochbrunnerschneide	Monte Popera	3,045	9,990
Gross Furquetta	Forchetta Grande	3,027	9,931
Sass Rigais	Sass Rigais	3,025	9,925
Torre di Brenta	Torre di Brenta	3,014	9,889
Kesselkogel	Catinaccio d'Antermoia	3,004	9,856
Punta dell'Uomo	Punta dell'Uomo	3,003	9,853
Grosse Zinne	Cima Grande di Lavaredo	3,000	9,843

ALPINE HUTS

GRÖDEN DISTRICT	GARDENA DISTRICT
Regensburgerhütte	Rifugio Firenze
Schlernhaus	Rifugio Monte Pez
Langkofelhütte	Capanna Vicenza
Sellajochhaus	Albergo Passo Sella
Bambergerhütte	Rifugio Boé
Pisciaduhütte	Rifugio Pisciadu
Grödnerjochhospiz	Albergo Passo Gardena
ROSENGARTEN	CATINACCIO
Grasleitenhütte	Rifugio Bergamo
Vajolethütte	Rifugio Vajolet
Sojalhütte	Rifugio Gardeccia
Kolnerhütte	Rifugio Aleardo Fronza
Oestertaghütte	Rifugio Roda di Vael
MARMOLATA	MARMOLADA
Fedajahütte	Rifugio Castiglioni alla Fedaia
Contrinhaus	Rifugio Contrin
PRIMOR GRUPPE	SAN MARTINO DOLOMITES
Canalihütte	Rifugio Treviso
Pravitalihütte	Rifugio Pradidali
Mulazhütte	Rifugio Mulaz
CORTINA	CORTINA
Sachsendankhütte	Rifugio Nuvolau
Tofanahütte	Rifugio Tiziano
Dreizinnenhütte	Rifugio Antonio Locatelli
Zsigmondyhütte	Rifugio Mussolini, and now Rifugio Zsigmondy-Comici
Pfalzgauhütte	Rifugio Luzzatti
(Rifugio Principe Umberto)*	Rifugio Bruno Caldart
BRENTA	BRENTA
(Rifugio Dodici Apostoli)*	Rifugio Gabari
Tuckethütte } Rifugio Quintino Sella }	Combined as Rifugio Sella e Tuckett
Tosahütte	Combined with new hut as Rifugio A. Pedrotti alla Tosa

Note.—There are many other Italian Huts for which, of course, no Austrian names exist.

* Italian Huts renamed.

Bibliography

Alpine Journal, 1858 to date.
Travels through the Rhætian Alps, Beaumont, 1793.
The Dolomite Mountains, Gilbert and Churchill, 1864.
The Central Alps (Vol. II of *The Alpine Guide*), John Ball.
The Eastern Alps (Vol. III of *The Alpine Guide*), John Ball.
Untrodden Peaks and Unfrequented Valleys, Amelia B. Edwards, 1873.
A Pioneer of the Alps, F. F. Tuckett.
The Climbs of Norman-Neruda, M. Norman-Neruda.
Wanderungen in den Dolomiten, P. Grohmann.
Wanderungen in den Ampezzaner Dolomiten, T. Wundt.
Bergfahrten in den Grödner Dolomiten, F. Benesch.
Baedeker: *Tyrol and the Dolomites* (1927).
Baedeker: *Eastern Alps* (1911).
Im Hochgebirge, E. Zsigmondy.
Über Fels und Firn, L. Purtscheller.
Die Erschliessung der Östalpen (3 vols.).
Alpines Handbuch (D. & Oe. A.V.).
Zeitschrift, 1874 onwards (D. & Oe. A.V.).
Illustrierter Führer durch die Dolomiten, J. Meurer.
Alpinismo acrobatico (*Peaks and Precipices*), Guido Rey.
Climbing in the Dolomites, L. Sinigaglia.
The Land in the Mountains, W. A. Baillie-Grohmann.
Tyrol, W. A. Baillie-Grohmann.

CLIMBERS' GUIDES

Da Rifugio a Rifugio, Touring Club Italiano, Milan.
Von Hütte zu Hütte (6 vols.), Verlag von S. Hirzel, Leipzig.
Der Hochtourist in den Östalpen, Purtscheller and Hess (Edn. 1927): Vol. VI, *Brenta*; Vol. VII, *Dolomiten*.

Dolomitenführer (3 vols.), Gallhuber, Vienna, 1929. (Also recently reprinted in one volume, which does *not* include the Brenta.)

Guide di Monti d'Italia, Club Alpino Italiano and Touring Club Italiano, Milan:

No. 26. *Dolomiti di Brenta*, 1949.

No. 29. *Odle–Sella–Marmolada*, 1937.

No. 30. *Sassolungo, Catinaccio, Latemar*, 1942.

No. 31. *Pale di San Martino*, 1935.

No. 33. *Dolomiti Orientali*, I, 1950.

No. 34. *Dolomiti Orientali*, II (in production).

MAPS

Carte delle Zone Turistiche d'Italia (1 : 50,000), Touring Club Italiano, Milan:

No. 1. Cortina d'Ampezzo e le Dolomiti Cadorine.

No. 5. La Val Gardena e i Gruppi della Marmolada, Catinaccio e Sella.

No. 6. Bolzano e ditorni.

No. 7. Merano e ditorni.

No. 10. San Martino di Castrozza e zone adiacenti.

No. 15. Gruppo di Brenta.

Touristen Wanderkarten (1 : 100,000), Freytag & Berndt, Vienna:

No. 16. *Westliche Dolomiten.*

No. 17. *Östliche Dolomiten.*

Index

Note.—Common descriptive nouns for peaks, alps, lakes, huts, etc., are ignored as a basis for this index, *e.g.* Lago d'Antorno will be found under *Antorno*, Cima, Brenta, Alta under *Brenta*, etc., doubtful cases being cross-indexed.

As far as applicable, both Austrian and Italian names are indexed, even though on the actual page one or other name may be used. Principal equivalents are quoted in parallel columns on pp. 94–6.

Text references are quoted first, in roman, illustrations second, in italics.

Index

Index